Agony of Dal Lake

Other books by Maharaj Kaul:

1. Meditation On Time
2. Destruction And Injustice: Tribulations Of Kashmiri Pandits
3. Life With Father
4. Inclinations And Reality: The Search For The Absolute
5. The Light Through The Woods: Dreams Of Survival Of Human Soul In The Age Of Technology

Agony of Dal Lake

Kashmir's Soul under Pressure

Maharaj Kaul

iUniverse, Inc.
Bloomington

Agony of Dal Lake
Kashmir's Soul under Pressure

iUniverse books may be ordered through booksellers or by contacting:

iUniverse
1663 Liberty Drive
Bloomington, IN 47403
www.iuniverse.com
1-800-Authors (1-800-288-4677)

ISBN: 978-1-4697-3507-8 (sc)
ISBN: 978-1-4697-3506-1 (hc)
ISBN: 978-1-4697-3505-4 (ebk)

Library of Congress Control Number: 2012900555

Printed in the United States of America

iUniverse rev. date: 02/09/2012

This book is dedicated to the people of Kashmir, who over several hundred years have suffered from numerous foreign invasions committed to plunder, kill, torture, humiliate, and rule them. They have also suffered from their own barbaric, selfish, and insane rulers and leaders. I am confident that they will overcome their present impasse and rebound with their customary tolerance for all religious faiths, care for the fellow human beings, simple pleasures of life, and love for nature.

KASHMIR'S SOUL UNDER PRESSURE

Oh! Kashmir your face is stained, your brow knitted,
There is a sigh in your voice, a hesitation in your step.
For eons you have been in this part of the world:
Paragon of beauty, icon of grace.
Now a defiled flower, a week shadow of gods.
Who has grizzled you with wounds, who has twisted your grace?
Enemies within have conspired to trade your soul in a bloody sport:
In a show of power, burst of passion,
Revenge of the ego:
A misconceived utopia, a blind dream.
Let me caress your brow, wash your wounds,
Let me dress you in love,
To reignite the old flame in you :
You will be reborn
And light the world around you again.

CONTENTS

E. Articles On Kashmir

F. Articles On Kashmiris

G. Poems On Kashmir

INTRODUCTION

A Long Enduring Heartbreak

Kashmir has been in my mind ever since I gained a consciousness to connect my observations with some sort of a thinking process. Obviously, it was due to my having been born there.

During my childhood I was ever conscious of the backdrop of the high mountains encircling me, no matter where I went. Also, life in Kashmir seemed to be secluded, a self-contained universe, with little interference from the outside. This contributed to the fairly-tale existence of my childhood.

Whether it was the enigmatic beauty of Kashmir, or my own inclination, which made me a thinker, I do not know. But my childhood was studded with a veil of mystery surrounding human existence. My growing up became a gradual unveiling of that mystery.

At the time of my birth Kashmir was a peaceful place, which from time to time was jolted by Sheikh Abdullah's assault on its undemocratic governance by the reigning Dogra monarchy. Kashmir went through the birth pangs of the new nations of India and Pakistan, but without being a part of the either. This orphanhood was self-inflicted by Maharaja Hari Singh. He harbored the fantasy of an independent nation of Kashmir. While he was going through the Micawberish state of mind, hoping for the best but without doing anything about it, Pakistan tried to exploit an inviting opportunity, while the Maharaja was in deep meditation on what to do and India was busy taking control of the reins of the new nation. It struck Kashmir under the camouflage

3

of a northern Kashmir tribal revolt against its government. Sheikh Abdullah, a staunch follower of Gandhi and Nehru, and latter's personal friend, had rejected Kashmir's integration with Pakistan and thrown its lot with India. Pakistani forces were stopped and repulsed to a point which left about one-third of Kashmir with Pakistan, when the U.N. sponsored truce was put in effect. Sometime after assuming the prime ministership of Jammu and Kashmir, Sheikh Abdullah recalled back his old fantasy of an independent nation of Kashmir. This situation of Pakistan's attack on Kashmir to absorb it and Sheikh Abdullah's change of mind about integration with India engendered the six-decade old intractable problem called Kashmir Problem. This was the beginning of the heartbreak of Kashmir.

Subsequently, Kashmir Problem became more and more unyielding, as the successive Indian central governments mishandled or did not handle at all the persistent viciousness of Pakistan in nullifying India's advantages over it of providing Kashmiris with a democratic frame of government, pouring a vast economic aid, and a hands-free approach to their government. Indian government was not able to stand up to Pakistan's shenanigans and Kashmiris' vacillation and week spine. Then there were incompetent and corrupt Kashmiri leaders, some of whom had divided loyalty to both the sides.

But what happened to Kashmirii people's common sense and sanity? Why could not they raise their hand for survival and decency? Why did they fall prey to Pakistan's Islamic card? Where did the wisdom of Lalla Ded and Nand Rishi go?

The Hindu-Muslim divide in Kashmir is more than 600 years old but there have been many long stretches of amity and peace between them. During the partition of India and Pakistan in 1947, when about a million people were killed, not a single person died in Kashmir. (Deaths in Kashmir in 1947 came from the Pakistani attack to grab it and not due to the partition) This accord between the people was not accidental but due to many efforts made by wise and common men from both sides over a long stretch of time. During the almost 500 years of Muslim rule in Kashmir there was never any serious attempt made to break Kashmir into Hindu and Muslim parts of the state or into two states. But exploited by the evil greed of Pakistan and seduced by the worldwide Islamic fundamentalist movement Kashmir Muslims lost their balance of mind and expelled the Pandits out of the Kashmir province.

The protracted experience of the Kashmir Problem has put heavy pressure on the soul of Kashmir. Kashmiri aloofness has changed to high-intensity partisanship, religious tolerance to extreme bigotry, and psychological tranquility to flawed passion. The present suffering of both the Muslims and Hindus will cast a deep shadow on their lives for decades to come.

Kashmir Problem has been on my mind since its phase-two inception in 1989. I have been obsessed about it. I have thought about it, written about it, and spoken about it. This is because it represents a violation of my sacred homeland, my birthplace, where the foundations of my mind were cast. Kashmir has been the scene of my childhood, boyhood, and early adulthood. Its desecration is a knife-stab through my heart.

The 20 articles on the Kashmir Problem were written over 21 years. They were started at the time of the inception of the present civil war in Kashmir in 1989. They were written as the state of mayhem, chaos, and exodus of Kashmiri Pandits, shifted from one peak to another, as each significant step for peace was knocked out, as each period of calm and constructiveness was shattered into hopelessness and misery by their enemies. The articles were meant for Kashmiris as well as for non-Kashmiris. They were written with anguish, at the moment of passion, but structured with a fabric of reason, and imbued with a lot of hope. Obviously, there is a lot of repetition in them, because though they were written at different times, they were on the same subject. They remind the readers that Kashmir problem did not have to have happened, if we had the right quality of leadership present at Kashmir and the central governments. Much frustration and heartbreak emanate from the articles, as I believed that the tragedy in Kashmir was man-made. At some point in future the problem will start attenuating, when we have the right leadership. This is especially more significant at the Kashmir end. Kashmiri leaders have been weak and corrupt, as they have let the masses bleed to secure their power and pages in history. A morally upright Kashmiri leader, concerned about the welfare of his people, would have arrived at a settlement with India a long time back. Throwing Kashmir's lot with Pakistan is suicidal and its independence would amount to the same thing, as shortly after achieving it, it would crumble into Kashmir's usurpation by Pakistan.

Kashmir people are not insecure about losing their land in their relationship with India. They are not insecure about practicing their religion of Islam under Indian nationhood. Kashmir cannot survive alone, as it does not have an economic base, and also it does not have the necessary military power to fend off Pakistan from usurping it. If its leadership had been honest and competent, as it was up to a point in the time under Sheikh Mohammad Abdullah, it would have continued to have an accord with India, as it did until August 9, 1953, when he was arrested for his separatist activities. Clamoring for more autonomy than what it already has is just an excuse for being closer to the state of independence. Islamization of Kashmir is another chimera of Kashmiris' troubled mind.

This book is about Kashmir Problem and vignettes of some of its places and people. Also, it contains 12 poems on it. The title of the book comes from the title of one of its poems *Agony Of Dal Lake*. Dal Lake is the most symbolic representation of Kashmir. Agony of Dal Lake is the agony of Kashmir. In the poem Dal Lake speaks about the pains, desecration, and humiliation it has experienced since 1989 due to the ongoing civil war among its children.

The heartbreak of Kashmir continues unabatedly. I do not believe it will be over within my lifetime.

Note: The articles and poems have been presented in the descending chronological order.

ARTICLES ON
KASHMIR PROBLEM

SIGNIFICANT MILESTONES OF KASHMIR PROBLEM

A. Pakistan Attacks Kashmir In 1947

1. Maharaja Hari Singh, the ruler of Jammu And Kashmir State, which was one of the 566 princely states in the British India, did not make a decision on whether to join India or Pakistan, the two nations that were going to be instituted after the end of about 200 years of British rule in the Indian subcontinent, as was mandated by the mutually agreed upon plan formulated by the Indian National Congress, Muslim League, and the British government. He remained without a decision even after Pakistan and Indian gained independence on August 14 and 15, 1947 respectively.

2. Taking advantage of Maharaja's indecisiveness and India's lack of seriousness in integrating Kashmir with itself, Pakistan launched an attack on Kashmir on October 22, 1947, under the cover of a tribal uprising against Maharaja's mistreatment of Muslims.

B. Kashmir Accedes To India

1. Maharaja Hari Singh not having the military resources to combat Pakistan's attack on Kashmir, and enemy forces having reached within a few miles of his palace, compelled him to seek emergency help from the newly formed nation

9

of India. Indian government advised by the governor general Lord Mountbatten agreed to help Kashmir on the condition that it integrate with India under the terms of the Instrument Of Accession, a legal contract formulated for the integration of the princely states by the Indian National Congress, Muslim League, and the British government. To the standard Instrument Of Accession contract was added a rider stipulating that when the conditions returned to normal in Kashmir, a plebiscite would be conducted to determine Kashmiri people's choice between India and Pakistan to integrate with. Maharaja signed the document on October 26, 1947 and Indian government sent its military to Kashmir to repulse the Pakistani invaders on October 27, 1947.

2. Maharaja made Sheikh Mohammad Abdullah, the National Conference Leader, who had been fighting him since 1930 for the equal treatment and economic advancement of Muslims, the head of the emergency administration of Jammu And Kashmir on October 30, 1947. He was an ardent follower of Gandhi and Nehru and staunchly advocated Kashmir's integration with India. He was made prime minister of Jammu And Kashmir state on March 5, 1948.

C. **India Lodges A Complaint With U.N. About Pakistan's Attack On Kashmir**

1. After having pushed the Pakistani military from Jammu And Kashmir up to point which left about 35% of it with Pakistan, Indian government launched a complaint with U.N. on January 1, 1948 about Pakistan's unlawful attack on Kashmir, which was now a part of India. Indian government also requested U.N. to hold a plebiscite in Kashmir to determine its people's choice between India and Pakistan to integrate with. Pakistan opposed the plebiscite.

2. U.N. declared a ceasefire to the war, which both India and Pakistan accepted, which was put in effect on January 1, 1949.

3. U.N. Resolution 47, on April 21, 1948, declared that in order to hold a plebiscite in Kashmir Pakistan will have to vacate its forces and tribal people in the areas of Kashmir which it had captured in the war and bring back the people who used to live there before the war on both sides of the present boundary, in order for them to participate in the plebiscite. India was required to withdraw its forces from the areas of Kashmir which it now controlled, leaving only enough forces to take care of the law and order. Pakistan rejected the U.N. offer to hold the plebiscite because it believed that it would lose it, and therefore no plebiscite was held. In 1990 U.N. dropped the plebiscite from its position on the settlement of the Kashmir Problem.

4. Governor General Mountbatten and Indian government several times tried to talk Pakistan into the plebiscite but with no success, as Pakistan feared that it would lose it.

D. Sheikh Abdullah Changes His Mind And Wants To Make Kashmir An Independent Nation

1. Sheikh Abdullah slowly drifted into an old dream of his of having an independent Kashmir. In that direction he clandestinely met representatives of foreign governments and projected a distinct coolness toward India. On August 9, 1953 he was arrested and jailed for his unlawful activities. In 1954 Jammu and Kashmir legislature under the leadership of Bakshi Ghulam Mohammad, the prime minister who succeeded Sheikh Abdullah, voted unanimously for Kashmir's integration with India.

E. Pakistan Attacks Kashmir Again In 1965 and 1989

1. In April 1965 Pakistan attacked Kashmir but was effectively stopped by India, the war ending with a U.N. ceasefire.
2. In 1989 Pakistan again struck Kashmir. In the beginning of the war Kashmiri Muslims sympathized with and helped the

Pakistanis. Almost all of the 400,000Kashmiri Pandits fled Kashmir and most of them ended up in the refugee camps in Jammu.

F. Present Situation

1. A British poll in 2010 indicated that only 2% of Kashmir Muslims wanted to join Pakistan. Majority of them wanted an independent Kashmir. Since President Musharaff rule Pakistan's rationale for having Kashmir integrate with it is that of Kashmir's Muslim plurality.
2. In all the elections since 1947 the majority of the voters in Kashmir have voted for pro-India political parties.
3. Many political parties in Kashmir continue to fight for Kashmir's independence but India's position continues to be that Kashmir has legally integrated with India in 1947 and 1954.

ETERNITY AND NOW

Self-inflicted Wounds In Kashmir

(September 28, 2011)

This article was written after my visit to Kashmir in August, 2011, after a gap of 11 years.

ETERNITY AND NOW

SELF-INFLICTED WOUNDS IN KASHMIR

It seems some places are destined to remain sorrowful, in spite of the best efforts of some of their people to make them otherwise. Kashmir is one of them.

Over thousands of years Kashmir has been a prey to the attackers from many foreign lands: Afghanistan, Mongolia, Turkey, Tibet. Sometimes I think that if Kashmir had not been as beautiful as it is, it would have had a more peaceful history than it has had, because its Shangri-La image has been an enormous attraction for the empire builders, adventurers, looters, and religious zealots. If Kashmir had been a place looking like any of the other states of India, Pakistan would not have vied for it with the same passion as it has. Kashmir's beauty turns it into a spiritual place, a clarion call for one's deepest religious or artistic sensibilities.

The majority of the local people of Kashmir started as Hindus, then changed to Buddhism, then reverted to Hinduism, and then changed to Islam. The history of Kashmir is tempered with extreme changes, long foreign occupations, extreme material lust, wanton killings, and religious persecution. A place pregnant with ethereal serenity and covered with enthralling beauty has been soaked with blood and hatred over many stretches of its history.

This contrast between Kashmir's natural and historical faces struck me with stunning intensity during my recent three-week trip there. The Kashmir of nature is still awesomely inspiring but the Kashmir of history is a wounded being, struggling to come back to life.

Dal Lake, a tapestry of tranquility and gracefulness, charisma and style, is both sensually intoxicating as well as spiritually tranquilizing. Its mystery and mystique transcends common understanding. It stands adjoining the other Kashmir, Old Srinagar, where a large number of people live. I visited its decrepit, mean streets, its rickety morose houses, punctuated sometimes with new houses, its abandoned crumbling Pandit houses. The creased faces of the people of Old Srinagar are etched with a million memories. They remember the revolution against the unfair Dogra rule, they remember repulsing the Pakistan government backed tribal attack of October, 1947. The promise of *Naya Kashmir* burned bright at that time. It was the first time in thousands of years that the political power in Kashmir was in the hands of its people. A new star appeared in the firmament of Kashmir, it was in the form of a tall, lean, and strong-minded Kashmiri leader named Sheikh Mohammad Abdullah, popularly known as Sher-i-Kashmir. In 1931, this born-leader challenged the might of the Dogra king Hari Singh, for equal opportunity for the majority of the state population, Muslims, with Dogras and Pandits. He also challenged the absolute monarch to change his government to a "responsible" government, which looked after the welfare of all the people and the integrity of the state. But his biggest war front was for the fair treatment of the landless peasants, the majority of whom were Muslims. His revolution in Kashmir ran parallel with the ongoing revolution for the freedom of India from Britain, spearheaded by Indian National Congress. He was mesmerized by its leaders Gandhi and Nehru. When the partition of India became a plan, he chose India to be Kashmir's partner, rather than Pakistan. He rejected Pakistan, on the basis that it was going to be a religious state, with not much care for the landless peasants, much to the bitterness and disappointment of its leader, Jinnah. His people unequivocally supported him in this.

A few years later the dream of *Naya Kashmir* started to unravel, as its chief architect, Sher-i-Kashmir, started to have another dream, that of an independent nation of Kashmir. Arrested on Aug. 9, 1953, due to his malfeasance, Sher-i-Kashmir's fall plunged Kashmiris into a new sorrow, so deep and intense that its shadows still haunt the people, even after its occurrence 58 years ago. Sher-i-Kashmir's dream of an independent nation of Kashmir was the greatest self-inflicted wound for Kashmiris. Even though, after regaining political power in 1975, after spending 13 years in Indian jails, he abandoned his dream, but the shadow of mistrust, engendered by his break-up with his commitment to Gandhi and Nehru, between Kashmiri Muslims and Government Of India, has remained a dark and impregnable cloud on the horizon.

Kashmiri history is replete with self-inflicted wounds. We let many foreign invaders in Kashmir, many without even a token resistance. Granted that in those times it fell to the ruling monarchs to defend the land, but the equanimity with which Kashmiris accepted the foreigners is deeply troubling. When Rinchin usurped the throne of Kashmir, the reigning monarch Sahadeva was hiding in Kisthawar, having given the responsibility of the defense of the throne to his commander-in-chief Rama Chandra.

After the end of thousands of years of rule by kings, sultans, and governors, many of whom were cruel, barbarous, cut-throat opportunists, plunderers, good-for–nothing rascals, racists, and nincompoops, we stumbled upon the incredible opportunity of democracy in Kashmir, helped by the Indian freedom movement against the British, in which the role of Sheikh Mohammad Abdullah was that of the chief architect. *Naya Kashmir* was the answered prayers, liberation from thousands of years of tyranny and slavery. What did Kashmiris do with it? They ruined it by the lack of scruples, greed, and blindness.

Within five years after Kashmir gained democracy, its chief architect started dreaming of an independent nation of Kashmir, whose feasibility he well knew was impossible. If the leader lost his brains, why did the masses have to lose them too? Kashmiri Muslims were also lured into the *Lotus-eaters* mood of freedom. What happened after that? Kashmir's relations with India soured badly. Who suffered the more in the test of the wills; of course, the Kashmiri Muslims?

In 60s and 70s Kashmir let itself be swept with the Islamic fundamentalism. Whatever happened to the famous Kashmiri sense of survival? Leaving survival far away, Kashmiris plunged into a suicide, they became contemptuous of India. Pakistan's attack on Kashmir in 1965 removed any illusions of the continuation of the 1947 status-quo between it and India. If Pakistan was really keen to have Kashmir, why did it not go for an all-out war for it, and extricated it from the greedy clutches of India? Pakistan was not willing to go that far, as it did not want to hurt itself that much. But why did not Kashmiris see the selfish and weak will of its suitor?

Kashmiris let themselves be drifted aimlessly, without embracing Pakistan fully, or without rejecting India fully. Can a people survive decently in such a double-handed game? Kashmiris have let themselves be humiliated, used, and mistreated by Pakistan. What happened to Kashmiris' honor and pride? Kashmiris lost their touch with the ground, floating in fantasy and fear.

In 1989 war with India, assiduously hatched by Pakistan over several years, Kashmiri Muslims fell for the call for the consolidation of Islamic people. They forgot that they could not win against India and that they were being used by Pakistan. The result, after twenty-two years of civil war, is that Kashmiris are isolated and hanging dry. They are living tormented lives, at the mercy of India and Pakistan, and losing their Kashmiri Pandit brethren. 400,000 Pandits ran for their lives, leaving behind their jobs, homes, and friends, and a culture woven over several thousand years, becoming refugees in their own country.

Kashmiris no longer want to merge with Pakistan, having come to know of its benightedness, but are now gripped with a demonic passion for an independent nationhood. They forget that their only genuine leader, Sheikh Abdullah, spent thirteen years in Indian jails without realizing it, ending up giving up that suicidal dream. Why have Kashmiris lost their capacity for reasoning? India cannot give them freedom, because there is not a single M.P. in the Indian Parliament who will vote for that. And for a good reason. Even if, hypothetically, Kashmir were given independence, any fool can see that within six months Pakistan will capture it. So, why would India give independence to Kashmir, when it would amount to handing it to Pakistan on a platter? Giving Kashmir to Pakistan is not an option for India, as it would bring the northern international border of India closer to its capital by 300 miles, and it will destabilize the 170 million Muslim community's ties with India. Also, the terrorist culture of Pakistan and its unstable political climate will be breathing closer over India's neck. Let us imagine that somehow India gives independence to Kashmir, which is followed inevitably, within a short time, with Pakistan's usurpation of it. Will Kashmir then call India to help it defend itself, as it did in 1947? And if Kashmir were to do that, would India oblige it?

Many idealists scream that people have an inherent right for freedom and that is why Kashmiris should be given it, but they forget that while a divorce between married couples is granted in many civilized countries of the world, but the mankind has not yet reached a state of development when a part of a nation can get a divorce from the nation. Once a part gets integrated with a nation, economically, politically, and militarily, and has historical ties with it, a separation is almost impossible. In exceptional cases when a divorce has taken place, it has been at the cost of a lot of blood. Kashmiris are not revolutionaries by any stretch of imagination. They have to make best of what they have. After 64 years of waffling it is high time for peaceful living.

Lots of different groups have suffered in the war of 1989: Indian military and Jammu and Kashmir Police, Kashmiri Pandits, and Kashmiri Muslims. But the group that has suffered the most has been Kashmiri Muslims. There have been families who lost their main providers, husbands and wives, sons and daughters, relatives and friends. The greatest sufferers of the calamity have to be the children. The children who were raised in the state of mayhem, gloom, and mental depression. Studies on the children of World War II soldiers have reported their constrained emotional and psychological development. The Muslim children will carry their traumas deeper and longer in their lives, compared to the children of other groups, because their traumas are magnified by the largeness of their group. They will grow with fractured emotions and stained psychologies. Such a heavy price for their parents' lust, first for a union with Pakistan, and then for independence. When a thing is impossible to achieve, how long can you keep on bashing your head against a rock? Young, bright Kashmiri Muslims will hit glass-ceilings when they aspire for higher level positions in their jobs outside Kashmir. For generations to come Kashmiri Muslims will be ostracized in social, professional, and political spheres outside Kashmir, because of the image of religious fanaticism and disloyalty toward India they have created by their war with it.

After my customary walk on Boulevard every morning, one day I decided to have my morning tea at Zabarwan Park restaurant, a government-run business. I found no customers in it, in fact I saw a man sleeping on the floor. I had just about-turned when I suddenly saw a man walking toward me. He told me I could only have a cup of tea at that time. We ended up sitting on a table in the lawn outside the restaurant, and started talking, without the help of tea. I was surprised that he opened the subject of Kashmir Problem. He seemed to be looking at a large historical landscape. He told me how Kashmiri Pandits were the original inhabitants of the Valley. He stated that they had to leave their homeland because of the recommendation of then Jammu and Kashmir governor, Jagmohan. I interjected his thesis by telling him how in 1989-90 Muslims commanded them to leave or else die. This rude awakening of his memory by me set him on a fairer assessment of the Kashmir Problem. He asked why there was so much army in Kashmir. I explained to him that the army was sent to Kashmir on Maharaja Hari Singh's request in the first place, when Pakistan attacked it in October, 1947. After Sheikh Mohammad Abdullah started cooling toward Kashmir's integration with India, after assuming Prime Ministership, Indian army had to be more vigilant. This was followed by *Mo-e-Muqqadas* episode, which was followed by Pakistan's 1965 attack on Kashmir. Most of the presence of army in Kashmir is due to Pakistan's continuing machinations. Had Kashmiris remained a steadfast partner of India and peacefully worked out their differences with it, the presence of army would have remained at about 1947 level, unless Pakistan had intensified its military posture at the border with Kashmir. Listening to the outline of the genesis of Kashmir Problem from me, he turned philosophical, and said what did Muslims get out of the twenty-two years of the civil war? Then he said wistfully that Pandits should return to Kashmir. He seemed to me symptomatic of a tide of the fresh thinking among some Kashmiris that their war against India was totally misconceived and had rocked their lives destructively. Another person I talked Kashmir Problem with, a lot more educated man than the earlier one, told me why was India so scared about holding the much ballyhooed and maligned plebiscite in Kashmir, as election after election, National Conference, a staunchly pro-India political party, had won the plurality of the votes?

The whole edifice of Kashmir Problem rests on airy columns of Islamic purity and consolidation of Islam round the world. Such ideals have no feet to stand on in the multiculturalism and internationalism we live in. The world is becoming a global village, where religious identity is no longer the highest level identity. Islam has never been difficult to practice in Kashmir. If there would not have been some foreign and a few local deluded, selfish, and vile hands exciting Kashmiris to religious fanaticism, they would have lived peaceful, constructive, and prosperous lives since 1947. Imagine how much happiness has been lost. A few rotten apples have turned the whole barrel into a malodorous and unsightly lot.

Gods gave a stunningly beautiful and bounteous land to Kashmiris, but they turned it into a political wasteland, a cancerous body, a sorrowful place.

Here are two faces of Kashmir: one eternally soul-uplifting and the other doomed by self-inflicted wounds.

> In the folds of Kashmir mountains resides the solemnity of gods,
> In the swirls of its breezes plays the music of the universe,
> Kashmir is the eternal enigmatic smile of God,
> Disturbed now by some selfish and rude outsiders and insiders,
> A dagger thrust in the grand design,
> My tears flow to wash its wounds.

(MK)

TO BE OR NOT TO BE

Kashmir Problem And its Two Architects: Jawaharlal Nehru
And Sheikh Abdullah

(May 1, 2011)

The article was written to clearly state the situations that created
the Kashmir Problem, and the roles two of its principal architects
played in it.

To Be or Not To Be

KASHMIR PROBLEM AND ITS TWO ARCHITECTS:
JAWAHARLAL NEHRU AND SHEIKH ABDULLAH

Little would Jawaharlal Nehru and Sheikh Abdullah know that Kashmir Problem continues to remain unsolved, in fact it has gathered the myth of one of the great unsolved political problems of the last 100 years of the human history. Nehru and Abdullah created the Kashmir Problem but they strongly believed at the time of its creation that it was solvable. Now time has imparted a hallow and mystique to it.

In the beginning was Jawaharlal Nehru, a Kashmiri Pandit, who greatly loved the land of his ancestors for its beauty, history, and the tug of roots it provided to him. By early 30's having become one of the high echelon leaders of Congress, he was in a position to impact the disposition of Kashmir, in the scheme of allocation of the 565 Princely States between the two new nations of India and Pakistan. The vested interest of Nehru was to play an important part in the development of the Kashmir Problem.

Nehru was born in an aristocratic family, so wealthy that they would send some special clothing to France for cleaning. After school and college education in England, he returned to India trained as a lawyer. His seven years of stay in England, at an impressionable age, had a lasting impact on him. His thought process, as well as dreaming, happened in English. Little did

25

his countrymen know that their great leader was quite a bit an Englishman in his thinking and lifestyle. The pursuit of a legal career could not hold Nehru's imagination; so after a short flirtation with it, he jumped into the ongoing movement for the independence of India from its 200 years slavery of Great Britain, under the compelling and enigmatic leadership of Gandhi.

Nehru was a student of history and was attracted to science; he had grown up to become an intellectual. These attributes held poorly against the Indian ethos of religion and mythology; Nehru was an agnostic and never visited temples on his own, except when political situation left no choice. He would complain that his countrymen did not respect facts, that is, facts did not much influence their thinking. Also, he was an idealist. This intellectualism and idealism combination got him into a lot of problems with his fellow political leaders, who operated with conventional wisdom. But he went on to burn his life at the altar of India, first for its independence, then for laying its foundation as a democratic nation. Little do many of his countrymen now remember or know that he was the chief architect of modern India.

Sheikh Abdullah was born in a family of shawl-weavers in Kashmir, in a cultural climate of Sufi humanitarianism; his grandparents were Kashmiri Pandits. His family having discerned in him early on a personality possessed of mental keenness, spared him of the family business, and launched him into an academic pursuit. He went to Government College Lahore and Aligarh Muslim University to obtain a B.A. and an MSc. in Chemistry, respectively. These were considerable achievements for a Kashmiri those days, particularly for a Kashmiri Muslim. He returned to Kashmir in 1930 at the age of 25and was hired as a teacher in a school. He tried to get a better job, commensurate with his education, but was thwarted in his attempts by the ongoing discrimination against Muslims under the Dogra reign. Unable to accept his and Muslims' condition as a fait accompli, he launched a civil disobedience movement for a constitutional and responsible government, which looked after all its constituents and not only after selected ones, which included generationally poor landless peasants. Only born leaders can defy circumstances and risks on their lives to confront authorities, that too which have absolute power, like Maharaja Hari Singh had.

Abdullah's party that launched the revolution against Maharaja Hari Singh came to be called Muslim Conference, which was instituted in 1932. Abdullah's towering physical personality (6' 1"), his mellifluous and fiery oratory, his revolutionary ideas, quickly turned him into a leader of stature, unlike anyone seen in Kashmiri history. His main fight was for the poor landless peasants, who were mostly Muslims, working on Dogra owned lands, and for uniformity of the laws of the land for all the people, and for the responsibility of the government for the welfare of its people. His renown spread all over India. While Kashmir was going through its revolution against Maharaja, India was already on that path over a much longer time against Britain. Abdullah learnt a lot from the latter. He felt strongly attracted to Congress because of its secular and idealistic policies. He stated that," . . . . people of Kashmir may attain their freedom in the larger freedom of India." He also believed his working class movement was above any communalism. He exhorted, "We must end communalism by ceasing to think in terms of Muslims and non-Muslims." With the advice of some people in Congress, but with the displeasure of Muslim League, in 1939 he changed the name of Muslim Conference to National Conference. When Congress launched Quit India movement, Abdullah launched Quit Kashmir movement.

Abdullah met Nehru in mid-1930's in Lahore and was immediately attracted to him on account of his idealism, keenness of mind, honorable demeanor, and personal magnetism. Nehru's being a Kashmiri was another factor of his hero worship of him. Together with Gandhi, Nehru provided quite a pull for Abdullah to throw Kashmir's lot with Congress, rather than with Muslim League. Besides the pull of the great personalities, he believed that Pakistan's strongest attraction for Kashmir to join it was that it was a Muslim state but he wanted secularism, which

Congress was strongly advocating for India. Also, Pakistan would be protecting feudalism and landlordism, fighting which was the raison d'être of his revolution against the Dogra rule in Kashmir.

Nehru's attraction for Abdullah lay in the kind of revolution he was spearheading in Kashmir for the benefit of the peasants and the common people, against the supreme power of a monarch. It was similar to what he was doing for India, only at a larger scale. Abdullah was only 27 when he ignored the risks to his personal life, inherent in such an undertaking. Furthermore, Nehru learnt about Abdullah's hero worship even in the remotest villages of Kashmir. He realized that his sobriquet Sher-i-Kashmir (Lion-Of-Kashmir) was apt. This was the kind of stuff that appealed to Nehru's heart and mind. They became personal friends.

Ever since the enunciation of the Two Nation Theory by Mohammed Jinnah, also known as Lahore Resolution, in 1940, which proclaimed that India was not a unitary nation, but consisted of two nations, one comprising Muslims and the other Hindus, Nehru had been anxiously watching Abdullah's revolution in Kashmir. This was because the heterogeneous composition of the state: Hindu king ruling a predominantly Muslim state, had the huge potential of creating problems at the partition of India. He knew his friend Abdullah was secular but he also knew the Muslim League, and the future Pakistan, would not like to lose Kashmir from its fold. Nehru's mind worked ahead of many other Indian political leaders in the uncertainty that was inherent in the situation of Kashmir.

In 1946 when Abdullah was arrested by Ram Chander Kak, Kashmir's Prime Minister, Nehru went to Srinagar to give him legal as well as moral support. He stated, "There can be no peace in Kashmir unless Sheikh Abdullah is released." Since Maharaja wanted to incarcerate Abdullah no matter what, he was. But to send a message to Maharaja, Nehru appointed Abdullah President of All-India States' Peoples' Conference, a body dealing with the people's affairs of the Indian states.

On June 3, 1947, Mountbatten announced that Britain had decided to divide India into two nations, India and Pakistan. A few of the 566 States, which occupied about a quarter of India, posed a problem in their being awarded to one or the other new nation, in that they had a heterogeneous composition: their kings and the majority of the people living in them were of different religious orientations. They were Junagadh, Hyderabad, and Kashmir. In Junagadh and Hyderabad the kings were Muslims but the people were Hindus. India argued strongly that it must be the people's choice that must decide which nation, India or Pakistan, they must join and based on that made a considerable effort for them to join it. But at the time of the partition of India into India and Pakistan, in August, 1947, the alignment of these states was still uncertain. Kashmir was the third largest Princely State, after Hyderabad and Mysore.

Obviously, Nehru had to maintain a uniform principal in fighting for the Princely States that had heterogeneous compositions. In Kashmir, unlike Junagadh and Hyderabad, the king was a Hindu but the people were Muslims. Prima fascia, it should have gone to Pakistan but what made the situation exceptional was the role of Kashmiri people's supreme leader Sheikh Abdullah. He was staunchly for India and had clear-cut reasons for rejecting Pakistan.

After the June 3, 1947 declaration of Britain to partition India, Jammu and Kashmir Government and those connected with it were thrown into a flurry of activities and all eyes were glued to it. Maharaja Hari Singh deliberately withheld his choice to join either India or Pakistan. This caused a great anxiety in Nehru, who knew a delay in Kashmir's choice would embolden Pakistan to lay claim on it. He wanted Maharaja to release Abdullah immediately so that the latter could tell the world that Kashmiris wanted to be with India and not with Pakistan. He wanted to go to Kashmir to help his case but Kashmir government did not allow him to do that. Frustrated, he asked Mountbatten to go to Kashmir to persuade Maharaja to release Abdullah and also gave him a 28 paragraph brief on Kashmir, written by him, to be given to Maharaja. In the brief Nehru pointed out that Abdullah was the preeminent leader of Kashmir, who was backed by National Conference for Kashmir's accession to India. So, freeing him from jail now would settle the matter of accession to India easily and that the alternative of Maharaja's joining Pakistan would bring him a lot of problems.

Mountbatten went to Kashmir to meet Maharaja between June 18 and June 23, 1947. He told him to take a decision to join either India or Pakistan immediately, but Maharaja remained non-committal. But asked Mountbatten his opinion on Kashmir becoming independent. Mountbatten replied that he thought Britain would not support it. He gave Patel's message to Maharaja that even if he opted for Pakistan, India would honor it. He also told him to have a Standstill Agreement with both India and Pakistan in the interim. Pursuing hard for Maharaja to make a commitment to join either of the two nations, but Maharaja's evasiveness pushed Mountbatten to the last day of his visit. The last day, June 23, 1947, came without any meeting taking place, as Maharaja pretended to have had an attack of colic. If Maharaja had not pretended to have colic and committed Kashmir, to either India or Pakistan, Kashmir Problem would not have existed.

On July 5, 1947 Indian government created two new departments called States Depts., one each for the new nations of India and Pakistan, which were to be born shortly, to facilitate the absorption of 566 Princely States between them. Patel was head of the India States Dept. So, getting Kashmir into Indian fold was his task. But as we have come to know, he was not for Kashmir's accession to India, as he did not have a lot of confidence in Abdullah and Kashmiri Muslims in this matter. He did not even respond to Maharaja's request for a Standstill Agreement. But history has shown that he was right. Because of Patel's coolness to the integration of Kashmir with India, invaluable time was lost in Maharaja's procrastination to accede to India and freeing Abdullah from the jail. Here was a study in contrast: Nehru thinking Kashmir was an asset to India and doing everything necessary to acquire it, Patel considering Kashmir a liability and therefore giving a short shrift to it. (Patel was considered having the necessary ingredients to influence Maharaja). Nehru wrote a letter to Patel on Sept. 27, 1947 (after India's independence, when Nehru was the Prime Minister) telling him his office had received information that Pakistan was making preparations to invade Kashmir. Pushed by his boss, Patel made Maharaja to free Abdullah two days after he received the letter. But nothing more happened from the Indian side for the next three weeks, when Pakistan attacked Kashmir on October 22, 1947. After release from the jail, Abdullah issued a statement," I never believed in the Pakistan slogan . . . . Pandit Jawaharlal Nehru is my best friend and I hold Gandhiji in real reverence." He went to Delhi and stayed with his friend, Nehru. If Patel had acted with passion and persuaded Maharaja to accede to India before Pakistan's attack, there would have been no Kashmir Problem.

Seeing Maharaja's vacillation and India's indifference to Kashmir, Pakistan attacked Kashmir on Oct. 22, 1947, with a camouflage of tribesmen, giving birth to Kashmir Problem. If Maharaja had signed the Instrument Of Accession before the attack, there would have been no Kashmir Problem. Once having been caught red handed with its hand in the cookie jar, Pakistan without any feeling of guilt or embarrassment, proclaimed that Kashmir belonged to it, by virtue of its believing that Kashmiris (96% of whom that time were Muslims) wanted to join Pakistan rather than India. But the irony is that when Pakistan attacked Kashmir, they had believed Kashmiris would lend them support and make the takeover of Kashmir easy, which did not happen, because they preferred India.

Pakistan's attack on Kashmir forced India to act, as Maharaja signed the Instrument Of Accession, and sent an SOS to Mountbatten to send Indian military help to thwart the invaders, as they were just a few miles away from his palace. Mountbatten strongly recommended the new Indian government to help Kashmir. Nehru considered the request coolly and thought that if the help were not provided there would be a bloodbath in Kashmir that would unleash mayhem all over India. Also, he thought he had to honor his friend Abdullah's request (who agreed with Maharaja's request for the Indian military help) to save the honor of his people. In Nehru's eyes Pakistan's attack on Kashmir was a barbaric violation of its sovereignty, which India must help Kashmir with, but there was no intention in it for India to stay on there. So, in spite of Maharaja's signing the Instrument Of Accession, Nehru believed that after the Pakistan's attack was vacated, it was for the people of Kashmir to decide which of the two nations they wanted to accede to. It was a very flawed thinking on part of Nehru, as he had the Instrument Of Accession and Abdullah in his pocket; he did not need anything more. The idea of holding a plebiscite after Pakistan was repulsed beyond the Kashmir border was preposterous, as at that point Kashmiri Muslims did not want to be with Pakistan; they wholly supported their leader Abdullah on this. Nehru's blunder was encouraged by Mountbatten, who independently thought of the plebiscite, and it was not opposed by Patel or any other cabinet member. What was he thinking when he came with the idea? Obviously, he was thinking of Junagadh and Hyderabad. He wanted to be consistent with the position India had taken on them, in that people's wishes had to be taken into consideration when dealing with the Princely States with a heterogeneous composition, when their kings and people had different religious orientations. But where was the doubt about Kashmiri Muslims' preference in accession? The proviso attached to the Instrument of Accession, referring to holding a plebiscite after the vacation of Pakistani attack and restoration of law and order in Kashmir, has created huge problems for India. Here was Nehru, keen on getting Kashmir in India's fold, but blundering terribly at the point of realizing his cherished goal.

Within twenty four hours of the signing of the Instrument Of Accession by Maharaja on Oct. 26, 1947, India launched Operation JAK, mobilizing an emergency force, comprising several hundred planes, and sending it to Kashmir. It thwarted Pakistani forces, when they were at the brink of entering Srinagar. On Oct. 30, 1947 Maharaja appointed Abdullah as the Head Of

Emergency Administration. After first denying complicity in the Kashmir attack, claiming it was purely a tribal invasion to stem the ongoing mistreatment of Muslims in Kashmir, Pakistan, later, when positive proofs of its masterminding of and participating in the attack were presented, confessed to its evil deed. The first meeting between India and Pakistan on the war was held on Nov.1, 1947, at Lahore. India offered the plebiscite, but shocking as it is to believe it today, Jinnah rejected it. Mountbatten's suggestion to have the plebiscite under U.N. was also rejected. Pakistan had made attempts to bring Abdullah to its side before the war. In Mid-Sept., 1947 it sent people to contact National Conference. In Oct. Abdullah sent Sadiq twice to meet the Pakistani Prime Minister Liaqat Ali Khan. The message from Abdullah was clear, that Pakistan should not force Kashmir to join it. Abdullah made the following statement on Oct. 31, 1947 "I . . . request Mr. Jinnah to accept the democratic principle of the sovereignty of our State, including as it does 78 per cent Muslims, whose free and unhampered choice must count in the matter of final accession." In other words, Abdullah was telling Pakistan that Kashmiri people had decided to throw their lot with India.

As the war continued in Kashmir, stories of the large-scale killing of non-Muslims and selling of Kashmiri girls reached Delhi, triggering intense reaction from many members of the Indian cabinet. They asked for an all out military punch to oust Pakistani and tribal attackers from Kashmir. But the military command, which still comprised of Britons at the top, after due deliberation, concluded that it was not feasible to do so. The reasons for that are not clear. It is said that Mountbatten had a role to influence military's decision, as he thought that all out war between the two recently formed nations would unleash a large scale bloodbath, which would destabilize the entire subcontinent, which was against the British interest. Mountbatten counseled Nehru that India must take the case to U.N., an inexperienced organization at that point, which had been formed only in 1945. For Nehru, inclined to be a pacifist and an internationalist, it was a good idea. So, India went to U.N. with the problem of the unresolved Kashmir war, with an offer, unbelievably, of a plebiscite. Pakistan neither wanted to go to U.N. nor did it want to have a plebiscite. Going to U.N., as we understand now, was the second major blunder Nehru committed about Kashmir. It is said that Patel, who was said to have been a lot more practical person than Nehru was, went along with the decision to go to U.N.

Just before Mountbatten left India for good, on April 21, 1948, he made one last attempt to resolve the Kashmir Problem: he proposed a partition of Kashmir, which Nehru accepted but Pakistan rejected.

Abdullah became the Prime minister of Kashmir on March 3, 1948;a crowning milestone in the life of a revolutionary, who set himself to overthrow its monarchy 16 years earlier. But being a revolutionary and being a Prime Minister are two different things. The difference is from being in a state of passion to a state in which one looks at things coolly. Abdullah's disenchantment with India began. It is not well understand what exactly caused it but it is thought he saw the signs of communalism developing in India, and his friend Nehru losing his backbone to fight it. Gandhi's assassination is said to have confirmed Abdullah's worst fears. As Abdullah's heart was cooling toward India, he tried to resolve the problem he was going to put Kashmir into. Since he did not want to be a part of Pakistan, because of its backward approach to the role of religion in the governance of a state, treatment of the poor peasants, and the evil attack it launched on Kashmir, that left only independence of Kashmir to resolve the problem. But nobody knew better than him how difficult it was to have that. He had many times in the past considered it and then rejected it due to the practical reasons. He had publicly stated that an Eastern Switzerland could not be created due to its being geopolitically unfeasible.

But Abdullah, in spite of his understanding that an independent Kashmir was impractical, could not let go of his dream. He was in a "to be or not to be" Hamletian state of mind. His meeting of some foreigners: Mrs. Loy Henderson, wife of U.S. Ambassador to India, some CIA agents, Sir Owen Dixon (U.N. Rep.), and Adlai Stevenson (two time U.S. presidential candidate) was interpreted by Indian intelligence to be his exploration of Kashmir's independence. On July 13, 1953 he said, "Kashmir should have sympathy of both India and Pakistan . . ." His statements and behavior with his colleagues and talks with Indian leaders lead to his arrest, removal from his office, and jail on August 9, 1953. This was very hard for his friend Nehru, who had to authorize it. He had written to his sister Vijaylaxmi Pandit, sometime earlier, in context of Abdullah's behavior," The most difficult thing in life is what to do with one's friends."

In August, 1953, after Abdullah's removal from Kashmir Prime Ministership and his jailing, Nehru met Pakistan's Prime Minister Mohammad Ali in Delhi and once again proposed a plebiscite to settle the Kashmir Problem, but with only one condition that Admiral Nimitz, the U.S. envoy to U.N., not be made the chief Plebiscite Administrator. This is because Nehru did not trust super powers like U.S. in this matter; instead, he proposed that someone from a smaller country be put in that position. But Pakistan, always diffident of winning a plebiscite, up to that time, made Nimitz's appointment a condition for the plebiscite. This was the last time when Nehru proposed a plebiscite to Pakistan. After Kashmir Assembly, on February 15, 1954, under the leadership of Bakshi, voted Kashmir's accession to India, Nehru believed that no plebiscite was needed, as the people had spoken.

So started the bizarre twist in the life of Kashmir's most ardent supporter of alliance with India. He was intoxicated by his dream of an independent Kashmir, whose emperor he would be. Practical difficulties of doing that, which had visited his mind several times, were swept aside by the intensity of his fantasy. He went on to spend some 13 years in Indian prisons. Did he have remorse for his actions, nobody knows? People like Abdullah, people of intense passion, never doubt their passion. His friend Nehru, who had to authorize the first two segments of his sentence, amounting to about 10 years, may not have been fully convinced about Abdullah's illegal activities, but he had no way of refuting the evidence his colleagues had collected against him. But as Kashmir Conspiracy case launched against Abdullah and others by the government was not brought to the court for several years, Nehru's conscience was bothered for the continued incarceration of his friend. (While the Kashmir Conspiracy case was later withdrawn for want of strong legal weight, nobody has any doubt that Abdullah's political misbehavior demanded his removal from his office). Abdullah was released on April 8, 1964. Right after his release from the prison he was the guest of honor at his friend's residence. It is incredible how a person who was punished by10 years of jail for his illegal activities by the government, could right after his release be the guest of honor at the home of the head of the government. It shows the unusually idealistic nature of Nehru. In his mind, in spite of Abdullah's mistakes, he was still a good man and good for the solution of the Kashmir Problem, and sent him to see Pakistan's President Yahaya Khan, with a proposal of launching a confederation of India, Pakistan, and Kashmir (an idea developed by Abdullah). Nehru obviously believed Pakistan had a role to play in the solution of the Kashmir Problem. Yahaya Khan rejected the proposal out of hand. Nehru died on May 27, 1964 and Abdullah publically cried for him.

Abdullah was rearrested on May 5, 1965, after Nehru's death, for communicating with China and Pakistan on Kashmir's independence, while he was abroad attending a conference. He spent another two and a half years in prison, being freed on December 8, 1967. Throughout his time in prison, starting in 1953, and out of it, before he regained his political office, he acted as the leader-in-exile for the Kashmiri Muslims who were disillusioned with India and were either seeking to accede to Pakistan or become an independent nation. He resurrected the bogey of plebiscite to his full advantage. It was his hidden as well as an open weapon against India. He was a staunch ally of India until he got the political power of Prime Ministership; after that his loyalty to India slowly eroded. Throughout his years of revolt against Maharaja and until sometime after he became the Prime Minister, he had no doubt that there was no necessity of a plebiscite, as he and his people were fully for the accession to India. After he was released from jail on September 29, 1947, he went to Delhi and met Nehru. Coming to know that Nehru was thinking of requiring holding a plebiscite a condition of Kashmir's accession to India, he told him that it was absolutely unnecessary.

Abdullah was made of steel, which was provided by his powerful ego, passionate nature, and religious zeal. Martyrdom appealed to him; but he did not care for principles or consistency. He knew his place was secure in the folklore of Kashmir and its history. In 1975 he reached a closely negotiated settlement with Indira Gandhi and became the Chief Minister Of Kashmir for the next seven years, dying on September 8, 1982, while in that position. During this period he renounced the dreams of independence and therefore of plebiscite. But by his unleashing of the genii of plebiscite, and playing with it for a decade and a half, he corrupted the psychology of Kashmiri Muslims' faith in India forever.

Nehru's idealistic streak made him commit blunders about Kashmir. In the beginning he thought that the requirement of plebiscite in Kashmir was necessary, even though Abdullah had assured him that there was no need for it, so that he could show Pakistan and the rest of the world that India was not usurping Kashmir but on the contrary Kashmiris were acceding to India in full volition and without fear. He would have seen to it that such a plebiscite was conducted but with Pakistan's attack on Kashmir the conditions for such a process taking place had changed, making its feasibility impossible. With one third of Kashmir under Pakistan how could a plebiscite be held? Even if it were held, Pakistan would not accept its expected results of favoring India, on the ground that the intimidation of Indian army toward the people made the result intrinsically biased. When U.N. Resolution 47, on April 47, 1948, required Pakistan to withdraw its military from Kashmir for the plebiscite to take place, it did not comply. Nehru's idea of continuing to offer plebiscite to Pakistan even beyond this point was that he wanted to be transparent, and he had nothing to be worried about, as he knew the results would favor India. But since there were practical difficulties of holding a plebiscite, he should have withdrawn the plebiscite card. By keeping it in circulation as long as he did, he created a psychology of uncertainty among Kashmiri Muslims, as they saw their leader Abdullah's bond with India loosen. Similar idealistic thinking on part of Nehru took him to U.N., after Indian military high command, in 1947, decided against an all-out attack on Pakistan. Nehru could have waited a little longer and let the British generals heading the Indian military that time leave India, and then have his way. By internationalizing the problem, he gave Pakistan and Kashmiri Muslims a card to play, even though it was blank.

Nehru's continued faith in Abdullah, even after he was jailed for 10 years for exploring the independence of Kashmir, was another practical error he committed. Abdullah, he should have known by then, was not fully loyal to India, as he had another agenda for Kashmir in his mind.

Holding a plebiscite in Kashmir, since it was first offered by Mountbatten and Nehru, in the Instrument Of Accession, that was signed by Maharaja Hari Singh, on Oct. 26, 1947, has remained a mirage. For more than a decade and a half Pakistan rejected it, because it feared its verdict. Later when Abdullah started dreaming of independence, Pakistan thought that it would favor it. Whatever double-minded thinking Kashmiri Muslims might have had about Pakistan in 70's through 90's, it is over by now. People have been turned off by Pakistan's weakness as a government and a society. Elections in Kashmir have repeatedly been in favor of politicians leaning toward India. The British poll last year, conducted by Royal Institute Of International Affairs and King's College, London indicated that only 2% Kashmiri Muslims would like to accede to Pakistan. Since Musharaff's presidency of Pakistan, it has withdrawn plebiscite as a requirement to solve the Kashmir Problem. Its raison d'être for having Kashmir now is that it belongs to Pakistan because of its Muslim majority.

Here were two persons, Nehru and Abdullah, both passionate and willful leaders, both intensely loving Kashmir. But one was an intellectual, an idealist; the other was a dreamer, soft on principles, opportunistic. The bad decisions of both of them on Kashmir have woven a fabric studded with pain, strife, distrust, bad dreams, and uncertainty, which continues to make the life of Kashmiris, both Muslims and Hindus, who live inside Kashmir and outside it, stained with sorrow.

THE IMPASSE
OVER KASHMIR

(December 9, 2010)

The legality of Kashmir's accession to India and its present demand for independence are discussed.

THE IMPASSE OVER KASHMIR

The impasse over Kashmir over time has proved to be painful, stubborn, and mythical. Kashmir watchers often wonder why a simple situation grew up to be so intractable.

The problem of Kashmir is the problem of a community changing its mind about its belonging to a nation it had been part of for several decades and the nation not being in a position to grant the community the independence it wants.

Beginning at the very beginning of the India Kashmir nexus, we go to the momentous event of the division of the Indian subcontinent into the two nations, India and Pakistan, in 1947. The division, among other things, involved some 566 states, the rulers of which had the option of either going to India or to Pakistan or in a special case remaining independent. (The people of the states had no choice in the matter). The king of Kashmir, Maharaja Hari Singh, asked the two nations to give him time to make his choice, what was called the Standstill Agreement. Pakistan granted it while India did not respond to it. While Hari Singh was still making up his mind, Pakistan broke the Standstill Agreement, and invaded Kashmir on Oct. 21, 1947. On Oct. 26th Hari Singh sent an emergency request to Louis Mountbatten, then the Governor General of India, to help him. Along with the request for the help he signed the Instrument Of Accession, without which he knew India could not help him. Instrument Of Accession was a legal framework for the accession of the princely states to India and Pakistan. It was accepted by Mountbatten on Oct. 27th and he requested the newly formed Indian government to help Kashmir.

The Indian troops were dispatched to Kashmir on the same day. Jawaharlal Nehru, India's Prime Minister, further stipulated that when the peace and order was restored in Kashmir, its people approve their state's accession to India, even though it was not required by the Instrument Of Accession. In 1952 and again in 1957 the Jammu and Kashmir Constitution Assembly ratified it. Furthermore, this willful choice was made under the leadership of the greatest Muslim leader in the modern Kashmiri history, Sheikh Mohammad Abdullah.

Nehru approached U.N. in Dec 1947, when the Indian troops had repulsed the Pakistani army only partially, to seek its intervention to get Pakistan out of Kashmir. This is considered to have been a monumental blunder by him, as he could have pushed the invaders all the way from Kashmir and then gone to U.N., if at all that was necessary. His idealism was so strong and his practical grasp of the situation so poor that he further jeopardized India's interests by asking the U.N. to hold a plebiscite in Kashmir to ascertain its people's wishes on which nation they wanted to join. Pakistan did not fulfill the U.N's. conditions to hold the plebiscite because it thought it would lose it.

So, Kashmir's accession to India has been without duress and absolutely legal.

Then why did Kashmiri Muslims change their mind in 1989 when they helped Pakistan in launching a massive revolt in Kashmir? The answer to that question lies in the unrelenting drive Pakistan has desperately managed to keep to acquire Kashmir, to divert the attention of its people from its monumental failures in solving their problems of economy and maintaining a democratic and stable government. Political leaders of Pakistan have reached an understanding a long time back that keeping the Kashmir Problem alive was vitally significant for their nation's survival. Through lies and mythologizing Kashmir has become a dream for Pakistanis, whose fulfillment would erase all their previous failures and make them pure once again and earn them a cathartic victory. Pakistan has invested hugely in keeping Kashmir destabilized over the decades, so that its arch enemy India's hands are not free to interfere in their nation. Also, the worldwide upsurge of Islamic fundamentalism has seduced Kashmiri Muslims into breaking their lot with India. Even though they prospered as never before in their history after they took over Kashmir in 1947, still their intrinsic religious insecurity made them double-minded about their relationship with India. They liked India's money and its pampering of them but their heart was with the Islamic center of gravity. In the earlier phase of their cooling of relationship with India, in early 60's, they wanted to join Pakistan; but in the last few years, seeing Pakistan's hopelessness as a nation, they have pinned their hopes on becoming an independent nation.

Pakistan's claim on Kashmir is based on the fact that the majority of Kashmiris are Muslims. Well, that is so only in Kashmir province. The state has three distinct provinces in it based on the demographics, history, and geography: Kashmir, Jammu, and Ladakh. Disregarding the areas lost to Pakistan and China, Kashmir has only 46% of the land area of the state and about 54% of the population. Jammu has 66% of its population as Hindus, Ladakh 50% Buddhists and 44% Muslims. Only in Kashmir Muslims have a majority of 95%. Both Jammu and Ladakh do not want to break away from India.(Ladakhi Muslims are different from the Sunni Muslims of Kashmir) So, no one is thinking of making the entire state of Jammu and Kashmir as an independent nation, even though in the entire state Muslims have a majority of 67%; only Kashmir province can be considered for that. The famous Kashmir Valley, where the majority of the Muslims live, has only 7.5% of the area of the state.

Whatever the reason for Kashmiri Muslims' change of mind, it is not easy for a nation to let a part of it sever from it. There are only a few examples of nations letting parts of it cede into new nations. Generally, nations consist of many parts which are intrinsically interconnected by history, culture, economy, and geography. Letting a part break away is difficult due to the emotional and practical reasons. Giving up Kashmir will entail huge difficulties to India. Foremost is the example it will set for some other restive parts of India, like Punjab and Assam, even though their active struggles to be independent of India are behind them but the old ambitions may be still be simmering in their peoples' hearts and minds. Also, Kashmir's breakup from India will send wrong signals to its 170 million Muslims. Then there is a massive concern for the security. With Kashmir detached from India, the northern international border of India will be some 300 miles closer to New Delhi.

Let us think for a moment that Kashmir is given independence. In less than 6 months from the onset of that Pakistan will doubtless invade it and claim it on the basis that they have cited for over the last six decades in its attempts to acquire it–that the Kashmiri Muslims want to join them. Nothing in the world at that point can reverse their usurpation. And the thought of that nightmare shakes Indians to even consider the independence of Kashmir. There is not a single member in Indian Parliament, which has the ultimate authority to let Kashmir cede from India, who is for it. Autonomy is the closest thing to independence that can be granted to Kashmir which is feasible. But Kashmir already has an autonomy provided by the Article 370 of the India constitution, which barring foreign affairs, defense, finance, and communications, lets it administer itself more freely than any other state in India can do it. Kashmir has even its own constitution and flag. All that is viable is to increase this autonomy.

So, unfortunately there are not many choices there are to cater to the wishes of Kashmiri Muslims. They are like married to India in a system of marriage where a divorce is not permissible. Will a time come in the future course of the humankind when a state within a nation can get a divorce from it as a matter of right? While the humankind is getting more and more sensitive to freedom, both individual and group, even a 100 years from now, I do not think that kind of divorce will be easy. Kashmiri Muslims, unfortunately, will have to shed a lot of blood for it. But we can ask the most germane question of the subject of the impasse over Kashmir: what is the need for Kashmiri Muslims to divorce India? They have more freedom than any state has in India; they are economically better off than most of the states; they have an absolute freedom to practice their religion. Just because the notion of Islamic exclusiveness crept in their minds sometime after 1947, must they burn up all their bridges with India, which in all likelihood will never grant them independence? In all likelihood, a few years from now, one of the pro-Hindu parties in power in New Delhi will remove the artificial oxygen protection of Article 370 to Kashmiri Muslims and let them live naturally like the rest of the nation. Their son-in-law treatment will evaporate and they will then rue why they had to rock their good life. The present Muslim leaders in Kashmir are leading their followers astray in a dangerous direction, after having already lost a lot of them in their confrontation with India, in which their trustworthiness by Indians will haunt them for decades to come.

THE KASHMIR PROBLEM

(April 21, 2010)

The article was written after the eruption of turmoil in Kashmir, which later spilled over to Jammu, over the transference of land, at Baltal, Kashmir, at an elevation of 11,860 ft., by the State government to Amarnath Sangarsh Samiti, an organization that had been managing the annual pilgrimage to Amarnath Cave for several years, to facilitate its work.

THE KASHMIR PROBLEM

Kashmir is like a very beautiful but a wounded woman. For a long stretch of its history it has been coveted and ruled by many foreigners. Immense misery has been wrought on its inhabitants by the usurpers. Even today, its neighbor, Pakistan, believes that it has the right to own it. Kashmir Problem has aged enough over its sixty years, without permitting a clear view to many of its observers of its solution, thereby maturing to have become an enigma. Several thousand Kashmiris have died, many more wounded, and a lot more displaced from their homes in the wake of the war, terrorism, and hatred Kashmir Problem has engendered. Above these images of Kashmir lie dark clouds of ignorance on the genesis of the Problem. Pakistanis and many people in the West believe that India is illegally occupying Kashmir.

Why is the problem so intractable? Only because of Pakistan's obstinacy to accept the facts. The facts are that in 1947, the year both India and Pakistan became free from Britain, Indian princely states had to make a choice of either being with India or Pakistan (a new nation being created). The choice had to be made by the ruling king of the state and its people had no say in the matter. There were 566 kings involved. Because Maharaja Hari Singh of Jammu And Kashmir was known to be an arrogant and a difficult person to deal with, the Indian leader, Sardar Patel, and the Govt. Of India's administrative executive, V.P.Menon, who were in-charge of managing the eligible states through the process of integrating with India, decided not to woo him to the India's fold. A special legal document called Instrument

Of Accession was created for the purpose of states' integration with both India and Pakistan. The initial vacillation of Maharaja Hari Singh melted fast after the Pakistan army backed civilians attacked Kashmir, exposing the thinness of Maharaja's military strength. He approached the Viceroy Of India for help, who in turn asked Prime Minister Jawaharlal Nehru to intervene. Indian Government approached Maharaja Hari Singh telling him that that they would help him if he signed the Instrument Of Accession. Maharaja accepted the condition, creating the bedrock of Jammu And Kashmir's accession to India. It is as legal as anything can be. Meanwhile, India went to U.N. complaining about Pakistan's unlawful incursion into Kashmir. U.N. declared a ceasefire which both India and Pakistan accepted. In the later negotiations in U.N. a move to hold plebiscite in Kashmir was passed but with the condition that the area of Kashmir presently under Pakistan (about one-third of Kashmir) should be first vacated and the people who originally lived there and had fled due to the Pakistan backed invasion should be brought back to participate in the plebiscite. (We do not know how U.N. will handle this matter now as sixty-three years have passed since the people fled the area) Pakistan does not talk at all about this condition of the U.N. plebiscite. Many young Pakistanis know nothing about it. Also, this is a condition Pakistan is supposed to have been reluctant to meet as it does not have the confidence that the relocated people will favor them in the plebiscite.

Subsequent to the above indicated event Maharaja left his state and he was toppled in power by Sheikh Mohammad Abdullah, a leader of the peasants and the common people, who had been fighting the Dogra royalty over several decades. He has been the greatest Muslim leader Kashmir has had. This was a single instance during the transfer of power from Britain to India that in one state indirectly a democracy replaced a monarchy. The new Jammu and Kashmir Assembly twice voted to have the state be a part of India. So, the integration of Jammu And Kashmir state was made legal three times. Subsequently, in the next two decades, the Muslims became the leaders in government, commerce, and culture. They had never seen such prosperity in their history.

But India's neighbor, Pakistan, was not only not happy with Kashmir's prosperity but also had deep designs of its own about it. Pakistan is a benighted country, where except for the first few administrations after its independence the government has been run by its military. Constitutions, supreme courts, and parliaments have been changed to suit a new president. One of the glimmering gems it has been dangling in front of its very angry and disenchanted people has been Kashmir. Politicians have been telling the people that the *jihad* with India over Kashmir was ongoing and sooner or latter they would be bringing Kashmir to them. Wars in 1965 and 1989 were the offshoots of this thinking. Kashmir is a well developed intelligence base of Pakistan. Pakistan has spend over half billion dollars over years to seize Kashmir. But this has not happened because of the superior military power of India.

The most important question about Kashmir is who does it belong to? The myth perpetuated by Pakistan is that it belongs to it by virtue of the Muslim majority of the vale of Kashmir, which is only a small part of the state of Jammu And Kashmir. No country can decide the nationality of a state of a sovereign nation. As has been indicated at the outset of this article that it absolutely belongs to India by virtue of the legality of the Instrument Of Accession which Maharaja Hari Singh of Jammu And Kashmir signed in 1947. It was followed by the state government run by the people's leader, Sheikh Mohammad Abdullah. Historically unprecedented prosperity befell Muslims subsequently. If India is sending military forces and otherwise spending a huge amount of money on Kashmir, it is because it is trying to defend one of its states. The matter is the graver as the people who are disturbing Kashmir are from the neighboring country who are bent on annexing it. It is an international crisis. Which Western country would sit silently and see one of its states annexed. Almost all the Western countries would be very aggressive in defending their territorial integrity. The Eastern ethos mold of India has rendered it into a passive country. If it had defended Kashmir aggressively earlier then perhaps it would not have seen Pakistan's war on Kashmir in 1989.

The recent eruption of turmoil over Jammu And Kashmir government's transference of some 90 acres of land to a Hindu organization called Shri Amarnath Sangarsh Samiti for annually facilitating thousands of Hindu pilgrims' journey to the Amarnath cave, a high level religious event. This was done because the government thought the organization would do a better job in constructing temporary shelters and other facilities for the pilgrims than it has been doing for a long time. The Muslim politicians seized upon this land transfer as a dilution of demographics between the Hindus and the Muslims and launched a bloody protest, which took the shape of the stoppage of work, food, and other amenities of living. In retaliation Hindus virtually stopped everything in the Hindu city of Jammu over two months, bringing the life there to virtually a standstill. The transferred land lies at 13,000 Ft. and so no one can live on it for an extended period of time. So, where does the demographic dilution lie? The Muslim agitation went beyond the land transfer to the breakup with India and joining up with Pakistan. Pakistan invests millions of dollars every year to keep the pot of unrest boiling in Kashmir. It also sends trained and armed infiltrators to achieve its goals. India has been rather weak taking the regular attacks inside its land in a low key, response as needed basis.

Unfortunately, there is a lot of ignorance in the world about Kashmir. The facts are that Kashmir is a legitimate part of India and it keeps military forces there to keep Pakistani infiltrators and Pakistani backed insurgents in check. India is doing a legitimate thing in defending its land.

THE ILLUSION AND THE REALITY

The Demise Of Kashmiri Pandit Culture

(December 7, 2005)

The article dwells on the eventual attenuation and demise of Kashmiri Pandit culture, as the ongoing civil war in Kashmir and the forces of globalization bear strongly over a small community with meager political and financial resources.

THE ILLUSION AND THE REALITY

THE DEMISE OF KASHMIRI PANDIT CULTURE

Walking down the fossilized time,
Crossing high pinnacles and green lakes
Of spirituality and learning;
Today the old native of Kashmir,
Kicked out of his natural habitat,
Wanders the far corners of the world–
To start a new life, a new community;
To heal his wounds, to follow the old light.

—m.k.

We are looking at Kasmiri Pandit (KP) community and wondering how long will it survive, as we have known it. Several years ago the question of survival would not have arisen, as the community was well anchored in its ancestral land of thousands of years. Although, it had changed quite a bit from what it was a hundred years ago, but no upheaval was expected–it was going through the natural modifications due to the ascent of the industrialization of the humankind and its socio-economic consequences. With the passage of the time there were also political perturbations in Kashmir strong enough to change a KP's position there from an indispensable intelligentsia in government service, education, culture, arts, and society to a second class citizenship, living on the circumference of these fields. But still he was in the land of his ancestors and the continuation of his culture seemed assured.

After the forced and substantial exodus of KP's in 1989 and beyond, the KP horizon trembled, and its future took a path of uncertainty. We are still on that shaky trajectory. What will happen to KP's as we have known them? This is a painfully significant question in the minds of the thinking people of KP community, whose answers are more often carelessly avoided than zealously focused on.

A community is a fine embroidery of history, culture, values, personality, myths, fantasies, and contradictions. A work of thousands of years of evolution and accident. When it is subjected to extreme pressure, it can start changing in some unknown directions. KP community experienced cataclysmic pressure in the political events of 1989 and beyond, such that its ongoing fragmentation is apparently hard to analyze, making it difficult to make a projection of its future. A withering impact suffered by a thousands of years old culture seems like a stellar collision in the outer space, where the shattered pieces of the stars, physically and chemically, can get modified to the extent of having no resemblance with their original character.

What the coerced and vast exodus of KP's from Kashmir unmistakably showed was that they had almost no political power there and they were and are sacrificial lambs when Government Of India (GOI) has a need to display its support for their arch nemesis Muslims. They also have had no economic clout for quite a while. The 1989 civil war was the tremendous explosion that shattered almost all the illusions that KP's had been harboring for decades about their security in Kashmir. For generations they thought that though they were are a minority, they still were respected by Kashmiri Muslims (KM's), (the majority community in Kashmir, with no love lost between them and KP's), and were independent enough to continue their legendary life in the fabled Valley. Any intelligent person could have discerned that their security was nothing but a thin veil of conventional politeness set up by KM's, ready to be cut asunder by them at a moment's notice. Why would an intelligent community like KP's fool themselves so long? The answer to this significant question lies in that human weaknesses can transcend reason. Human beings are often fooled by political and cultural realities, even though the concerned people possess good intelligence, because they do not want to accept the reality. KP's lived in a fool's paradise for a long time, thinking GOI would never forsake them. The lesson learned is that KP community intelligence is vulnerable like any other community's.

Since this KP diaspora has a high dimension and a finality to it, which makes it the most significant since the diaspora in the fourteenth century, under Sultan Sikander (1389-1413 C.E.), which was later reversed. What have the four hundred thousand refugees done since they were forced to leave their birthplace? Immediately after the exodus, most of them landed in Jammu Refugee Camps. At this point personal resources and the government allowance saw them through this period of great mental and physical anguish. Slowly, many of the refugees found jobs outside the state government, allowing them to quit the degrading camps. Over years, the camp population has dwindled to a few thousand. Many a young KP is said to be doing very well in his or her job outside the J &K Govt. Some KP youngsters were able to migrate to countries outside India. So, economically most of the refugees are doing all right, with good prospects for future growth. While the older KP "exiles" still suffer the pangs of separation from Mother Kashmir, youngsters, generally, do not feel the same way. This is because many of them had already fixed their dreams and goals away from Kashmir. In the decades before the civil war, the KP youngsters were already moving more and more out from the Valley, because of the limitations of the good professional jobs, unfairness of the Government, and the slow growth of the modernity. The civil war only gave a tremendous boost to the trend.

There are no more than 700,000 KP's in the world. Jammu has the highest KP population for one city. Not more than 30,000 live abroad. In most of the cities they live in, in India and abroad, they have a community organization, which organizes some of their festivals, and promotes interaction among them. There is talk among the older members of the survival of the KP culture. The younger members do not feel as much heartbreak in the demise of Kashmiri culture. This is because they have not had a strong link with it. Culture is a dynamic experience–either you live it or you are not in it. With the younger KP's moving out of J & K State for quite a while, for the reasons indicated above, the requisite dynamic interaction has receded. People living in large metropolises acquire a new unnamed culture, which is cosmopolitan, modern, and practical. This culture is based on the modern notions of the individuality, freedom to choose among various equally valid lifestyles, and to a good extent on the scientific perspective of human life. The younger KP's do not know much about the high achievements of their forefathers thousands of years ago. They do not have a good knowledge of how Kashmir used to be a Hindu, and later a Buddhist center of learning. That in ~1-2 C.E. 4th Buddhist Council was held in Kundalvan (perhaps the present day Haravan), which was an international conference, with about five hundred participants from many different parts of the world. Also, it was from Kashmir, the scholars of Buddhism traveled to different parts of the world to spread its message. Such subjects were not a part of their curricula in schools or colleges. Pride in Kashmiri heritage is downplayed while a KP is living in Kashmir, it only takes high value when he is out of it. The core of a modern KP personality is that of a practical person, focused on survival, competition, and materialistic success. KP children jump on this worldly road much earlier than their fathers did, because of much higher competition and individual dynamism that exists now than in their times.

Another significant factor contributing to KP children's coolness toward Kashmiri culture is that they are not being taught Kashmiri at home. A good number of KP's unconsciously feel the inferiority of the old life back home, and so they do not feel compelled to teach their children their ancestral language. There is this contradictory double personality in a common KP: on one hand he is unconsciously proud of his heritage, on the other he wants to keep away from it. Consciously, a KP wants to be a practical person, living in this world, with his feet on the solid ground below, and during these times. His pride for the old Kashmir and its culture is purely a tapestry hanging around his history, but of no practical value. A KP is not a dreamer or a preacher. He lives most of his time in the reality manifest by the material world. Young KP's generally take practical professions like engineering, business administration, medicine, and accounting, not professions in arts and research in various fields. They can not be called scholarly, philosophical, idealistic, or artistic in disposition. Surprising, even shocking, it may seem to many people to know that a good number of KP's are not truly religious. They possess a religiosity in some aspects of their lives, but they are not day to day practioners of the classic Hinduism. Most of them do not understand Kashmiri Shavism. Modern KP's are almost true non-conformists. So, the bonds of young KP's with the traditional Kashmiri culture are tenuous–more a projection of their social responsibility, than an inspiration in their minds and a thud in their hearts. Some young KP's in U.S. wondered in one of the annual KP Camps (organized by KOA), if not knowing Kashmiri made it difficult or impossible for them to be KP's. Although we know, from the experience of other migrant communities, that the lack of knowledge of their ethnic language did not prevent them from becoming that ethnic. Language is the deepest channel of emotional communication between an object and a mind. So, the identification with a group is much easier with it. Also, the younger people, more than the older people, feel the obstacles that community boundaries make in their sense of belonging to the more inspiring and enlightening notion of belonging to the humankind and to the world.

No group of KP's is larger outside India than the KP's in US. It is estimated to be 2000 families large, which is about six thousand people. The organization that binds them together is Kashmir Overseas Association (KOA), that was founded about twenty-seven years ago. It is the richest KP organization in the world. KP's in US donate about $ 75,000 annually to the destitute KP's, mostly in Jammu, mostly for the education of their school and college going children, and for the medical and economic calamities. Also, the fire in the bellies of US KP's for the plight of the KP refugees, and the propagation of some form of KP culture, is the strongest among all the KP groups in the world, including those in India. This has made KOA an organization to watch. GOI is aware of this, as is Pakistan Government. The KP groups within India lack the fire in their bellies and the cash in their pockets. From the much lauded Panun Kashmir group, based in Jammu, much was expected, as it was given the charge of influencing GOI to be more helpful to KP's than it has been. But it has failed to unite KP's even in Jammu, not to speak of the rest of India, or rest of the world, to present to GOI a strong group, which has been ethnically cleansed, determined to fight for what is their due. Such a failure has been very discouraging for KP's worldwide. They do not believe GOI can give KP's the kind of security they need, to those who wished to return to their ancestral homes, for living or for a visit. Majority of the KP's believe that for all practical purposes they have lost their homeland, even though it continues to be a part of India. So, having lost faith both in GOI and KM's, KP's are fighting hard to adopt to their new surroundings. The fight for the survival of their culture only comes after their survival for life, and that too generally among the KP's fifty or older. For younger KP's cultural survival has a much lower priority.

Life for KP's after Sultan Shams'd Din started a long era of Muslim rule in Kashmir in 1339, had been difficult, at times perilous, not conducive for a group formation. Particularly the persecution of KP's under Sultan Sikander (1389-1413 CE) (when KP's had to pay *Jazia* (tax) for not being Muslims and when they could not use a *tilak* on their foreheads, etc.), when they left the Valley in large numbers, to the extent that at one point only eleven families were left there. KP's have generally throughout their history, after Sikander's rule, been not good at being together on a sustained basis, to give their cruel rulers something to worry about. Most likely because of their numbers, lack of resources, and mental makeup, they could not group against their tyrant oppressors. KP's have more often tried to live with their problems (which can take a lot of character) than tried removing them. This sense of accommodation, right up to the modern Muslim rule in Kashmir, has not been helpful in their plight. No wonder, even today we find KP's hard to unite, to fight the common enemy together. Efforts to unite KP's world over as a cultural group so far have not succeeded. KP's see themselves more as individuals than a group. This personality dynamic is against the survival of their culture.

Recently, the KOA presidential election in US got so sordid because of accusations and counter accusations of the two dominant groups (West Coast KP's and East Coast KP's) that it was with sheer luck that KOA survived. Many people in the groups did not care for the survival of KOA but only for their egos and images. Similar things happened to Panun Kashmir in Jammu, resulting in a multi-group split, which obviously weekend the community. Fights within KP groups in some other cities of India and other countries of the world are not uncommon. All these organizations are poorly resourced and basically only serve the role of organizing the two cherished KP religious festivals of Shivratri and Diwali annually, and providing their members the opportunities of networking. So, what do the people fight on? Their interests, their egos, their images. If KP's do not have a group personality how can they fight GOI for fairer treatment of the KP refugees and more concessions for them and how can they carry on their traditional culture, both enterprises heavily exhorted by their leaders to work on? Conditioned by hundreds of years of persecution of the Muslim and Pathan rule, KP's ancient personality has warped, such that it does not trust a fellow KP in a group structure. KP's also generally lack leadership qualities. Both these lacks come from the high lack of the psychological security–a basic quality that is not easy to acquire and repair, as it needs sustained corrective actions, over time

Some KP's compare themselves with Jewish people, when considering their tribulations, gift for survival, and perpetuation of culture. Jewish people are lot more tenacious in fighting for their causes, have more resources, and are more in numbers than KP's, making them better in both survival and perpetuation of their culture. KP's are only three quarters of a million, while Jewish people about eight million. They are far, far richer than KP's. They have a tremendous group identity and have been fighting very hard for what they believe is theirs. We can not say the same things for KP's.

All communities in the world are changing because of the tremendous success of science and technology, big strides in political life, and economic globalization. The world is turning to a global village. The old concept of a community is changing. Man's self-image is changing. The incredible demands on the energy and time of modern man has forced him to abandon some of the old notions of family, work, society, and self. In the flow of change, KP's cannot afford to be behind other people. They neither have a political base nor an economic base, and the worldly cultural base they have, they are not sure if that can carry them through the world. But the spiritual base they have, they are more confident about it. To carry it on needs conviction, work, and resources, which they have a dearth of. Because of this, with time, their culture will effectively attenuate, leaving only its wrapper, when the gift within it has withered away. Community organizations can not hold the tide of change, unless they are committed, resourceful, active, and forward looking. Essentially, the cultural preservation must be a deeply held emotion among the people, for it to be effective. If the emotion is weak or missing, no amount of resources and community organization work will be able to maintain the culture.

The question is what will KP culture be like a hundred years from now? Some of the last names, after modifications, may survive in the KP world outside India, but the first names will be replaced with foreign names in most of the cases. Kashmiri language will not be spoken anywhere except in a few places in India (chiefly in Kashmir). Shivratri will be celebrated in foreign countries where KP's live, though with modifications. In India it will survive well, as it is also celebrated by other Indian communities. Kashmiri calendar will not be used abroad, but in India it may be used on a meager scale. Minor festivals will disappear. KP music will slowly fade away among the KP's living abroad. KP artistes will go for non-Kashmiri Indian music, while the Kashmiri music from the KP's and the KM's in Kashmir will be heard by a small number of KP listeners. Kashmiri Shavism will perhaps survive because of its philosophical appeal to some people in the world. Time will gradually kill many KP myths and much folklore, as it will change many social customs. A hundred years from now KP's will be integrated with the Hindus of India. In fact, KP's will call themselves Hindus, except for a small number of them still clinging to the name KP.

Einstein defined education as something that remains, when everything one learns at college is forgotten. Same could be said of culture. It is something that remains, when traditions, customs, festivals, and language of a group of people change. So, even after a hundred years from now, a person of Kashmiri origin may retain certain philosophical inclinations, social behavior, and tastes in arts, etc., as his forefathers did. But for all practical purposes most of the KP's after a hundred years will not be possessing the KP culture as we know it now. Some of the other groups like Muslims and Jewish people have made strong efforts to retain their cultures and the results show their success. If KP's were more in numbers, had more resources than they have, and had greater ambition than they have, KP culture would continue, although in a modified form.

> *Cut off from its spiritual center,*
> *The community wandered in silent grief,*
> *To find a mooring,*
> *To revive the luminosity that brightened its world,*

Maharaj Kaul

To rekindle the fire that bound it together.
But unable to be reborn,
It gradually drifted into the unnamed universal
melting pot,
Turning its hallowed past into history,
Its vision into fossilized hopes.

-m.k.

THE TRIP TO TOUCH
THE HALLOWED LAND

The Visit To Kashmir In 2002

(January 13, 2003)

The visit to Kashmir in November-December, 2002, after 14 years, created new perspectives on its human conditions by the ongoing civil war there.

THE TRIP TO TOUCH
THE HALLOWED LAND

THE VISIT TO KASHMIR IN DECEMBER 2002

I had been haunted and agonized by the idea that I had been unable to go back to my birthplace Kashmir for fourteen years. Darkly hallowing this idea was the anguish I felt over the death of some sixty thousand people and the driving out of the whole community of Kashmiri Pandits, the original settlers of the land, by a degraded and a dishonorable war, which has conflagrated the place for the last fourteen years and is ongoing, perpetrating the fraud of seeking to give Kashmir's Muslim inhabitants their supposedly long sought after freedom.

I made an attempt to visit Kashmir during my 2000 trip to India but was rebuffed by my flimsy planning, reinforced by half-willed ambition.

In 2002 I made good of my earlier failure, which besides other things meant riding rough-shod over well-meant advice and conventional wisdom of my relatives and friends to avoid this dangerous area. A plan to visit Srinigar, Kashmir was made and it was executed, enabling me to fulfill the long cherished longing of touching the hallowed land of my ancestors, my birthplace, and the site of my early adulthood, which now lay crassly defiled and its people deeply wounded.

The flight from Jammu to Srinagar, though of only twenty-five minutes duration, was choked with unshakable trepidation, stressed with over-controlled excitement, and buffeted with the slow release of cloaked longing. The sight of the Pir Panjal range of mountains was the sounding of the bugle of welcome to the Valley. Within minutes after the welcome call was the sight of the Valley itself–veiled with the thin veneer of clouds with enigmatic movement. The first look of the Valley at this point from the vantage perspective of the ten-thousand feet elevation is that of a semi-real place–magnificently contoured by mountains, the valley below diffused though panoramic. The sun was shining lavishly on this day in November.

The passage through Srinagar airport security was rather too smooth, considering the danger afloat in the place. My host and I recognized each other with electric intuition, though having never met before, and we began the drive to Amira Kadal, Residency Road, Bund areas, the grand piece of the mosaic of the city of Srinagar. There was a new road coming out of the airport. Looking at a distance one noticed new construction, something which warmed my feelings in that that in spite of the life crushing upheaval of the last decade and a half the emotion to live in the inhabitants of this place persisted strongly. Getting closer to the city the presence of military posts and their frequency was one certain sign of something having gone terribly wrong with this place. The traffic in the heart of the city was heavy, again giving the impression that life was going on, in spite of the horrific situation surrounding it. The Lal Chowk, the center-square of the city, seemed to be a washed out picture of its previous glory. Beyond it, toward Partap Park, the scene seemed even feebler. The Bund, the riverside boulevard, the heaven of the evening walkers, was completely deserted, its legendary shops, I am sure, were almost completely empty. Even accounting for the winter low turnout of people, the sight seemed mournful, more perhaps because of its contrast with its past grandeur.

Traveling through the core downtown areas, some of which I was seeing for the first time, I got the chance, which I greatly wanted, to have a glimpse of the surviving real people of Kashmir. In the dilapidated structures, often bereft of light and air, almost always without the modern amenities of life, live human beings who have taken the heaviest brunt of the brutality of the last decade and a half. These are the people who by now have forgotten which side of the war they are with. Some seventy-five years ago, a great son of theirs, Sheikh Mohammad Abdullah, fought for their freedom from their historical backwardness. In 1947 they were ushered in a new age of democracy, both political and economic. In the subsequent four decades they were transformed from landless tillers to landed gentry, from the lowest rungs of the social ladder to the top echelons of wealth and political power. But yet they were thrown into another fight for their freedom in late 80's, this time for a state based on their religion. But this fight proved to be very difficult, pulling immense sacrifices from them, and its conclusion is very much under a cloud as to whether they have any chance of winning anything of what they wanted.

The famous Kashmiri stylized walk, a picture of body coordination and intense self-consciousness, was still alive. People looked terribly preoccupied and yet seemed to walk with a purpose. They seemed not to socialize while walking. Behind their apparent calmness and focus they seemed to cloak something. What is on their minds, one wondered. Shops filled with packaged goods looked awaiting customers. Cars and micro-buses running with heavy punctuation of screeching horns and brakes, just always managing to miss pedestrians. A bizarre traffic scene, perhaps without a duplicate in the world outside India.

Frozen in time, the Srinagar downtown is a vibrant organism, where political and social emotions run deep and strong and primeval personality reigns. People are intensely involved with themselves and do not pay much attention to the other parts of the world. Their stubborn loyalty to their traditions, ideas, and emotions can not be bought off. The buck seems to stop here. Their stoic acceptance of their sufferings engendered by the political war in the area is sustained in good measure by their belief in the rightness of their political positions. The mixture of pride and stubbornness, non-conformism and fatalism, forms the essence of Kashmiri personality, which unfortunately has come to become an immense barrier in the resolution of the ongoing civil war.

River Jhelum is the centerpiece of the city of Srinagar, intertwined with the daily lives and the culture of its people. It is not sinewy like Seine in Paris or wide like Hudson in New York, but is physically more intimate with the surrounding habitation than them, like a street running through the town. During winter its water level falls significantly, exposing the unsightly shores. Three new bridges over the river have been added: Biscoe Bridge (south of the demolished Fateh Kadal), New Habba Kadal (south of the old but still used Hubba Kadal), and New Zero Bridge (north of the still used old Zero Bridge). I was told that the statue of Tyndale Biscoe which was erected on the west end of the bridge named after him was demolished by the local people, presumably on the ground that he as a foreigner was unacceptable to the sensibilities of Islam and their culture. Biscoe was a shaft of light in the Kashmir of early last century with his creative ideas on education and the school he left has continued to remain a gleaming institution of character building and learning. The topic of the bridges reminds me of another noble soul, Bad Shah, for whom Bad Shah Bridge is named. His official name was Zain-ul-Abidin, who ruled Kashmir from 1420 to 1470. His treatment of Hindus and tolerance of Hinduism was such that his reign is considered a high-point in the Hindu-Muslim relationship since the advent of Islam in Kashmir in 1339.

Driving down the Srinagar downtown sights of the burnt Hindu houses are frequent. It is amazing to see the precision with which the fires have been extinguished just at the boundaries of the targeted houses, leaving the adjacent houses intact. Most of the burnt houses have not fully burnt, leaving the wooden structural members and the masonry at precarious positions, posing safety risks. Either Government has thought the posed danger to be insignificant or has not thought at all. The thought comes of what were the Muslim onlookers doing when the militant targeted houses were burning. The inhabitants of the adjacent or adjoining Muslim houses must have been tearing with fear of their houses catching the fire. But most likely the fire starting people must have taken care of the situation and assured the Muslim neighbors that their houses will remain safe. Also, frequently visible were the shuttered up Hindu shops which, most of them, I was told, had been by now sold to Muslims. What do Muslims feel and think when they see amidst them the burnt houses and the shuttered down shops?

There are much lesser number of people walking on the streets than before. This can be explained as an enormous number people have died, almost the entire Kashmiri Pandit community has emigrated out, and a lot of Muslim young people have also emigrated out of Kashmir, many of them going to the Middle East. The downtown looks like a semi-deserted town, with little excitement and cheer; everything seems gray, solitary, and feeble. Where is the hustle and bustle of Habba Kadal, the tension on the streets, the excitement of the school children, the energetic solicitation of the shopkeepers, the aggressive haggling of the shoppers? The acute shortage of electric power resulting in its daily rationing does not help the stained ambiance of the place. The semi-lifelessness of Srinagar and environs, and we can venture to stretch this condition to the entire Valley, is emblematic of the decade and a half long barbaric activities in the area. The Kashmir Valley is a humanized prison-camp.

I ventured into the old Fateh Kadal area to see my ancestral home at Malik Yar. This place is now close to the new Biscoe Bridge, which replaced Fateh Kadal. Kauls had lived at Malik Yar for generations in a compound comprising several houses, which in its heyday may have amounted up to nine families. Now there was no one of them living here, though most of the buildings appeared to be on the ground. (In fact a new building had arisen on a compound, which was used as a playground by the children). A black patina had grown over some of the buildings, an effect accumulated by time. The complex seemed to echo loneliness and abandonment, neglect and unhappy times for the people living in it. I introduced myself to some young women who careened out of the windows to sight the stranger standing in their compound and photographing the structures. They appeared to be defensive in their being the new occupants of the buildings, which were once owned by my families, saying that they had moved from the immediate neighborhood. Some of the neighbors, whom I had known since the early adulthood, came out of their windows inquiring about the welfare of my other family members and inviting me to tea, a customary gesture of welcome and friendship in Kashmir and many other parts of India. I was amazed to see how even the long stretches of silence among neighbors had not dulled their ardors of friendship. Some human relationships can defy the dilution and disintegration engendered by the unwearied assault of time. Scenes of my childhood flashed in a stream of consciousness mode through me: playing, going to school, fear of elders, excitement on festivals and weddings, growing awareness of mystery of life and efforts to keep it cloaked from others, lest I be taken as a lunatic (a fear which has not completely left me even now). I tore myself from the physical backdrop of my early life as prolonging the stay, I thought, might cause a stir in the neighborhood leading to some problems with the militants. As I left I thought someday I needed to return here in greater inner tranquility to contemplate my early life and the growth of my consciousness.

From the old Fateh Kadal area I moved to Karan Nagar, not a downtown area, and also not an old area, inhabited mostly by middle and some upper class people, mostly Hindus. It appeared to be mostly intact, viewed from its central boulevard. Furthermore, new shops have erupted in its northern section. Here I looked for my uncle's home, where I had spent a lot of time. It had become my home too as my father moved from country to country as a professional diplomat. The house was sold by my uncle in 1999. The new owner owned it for a short time only, demolishing it to construct a diagnostic center, which is a much bigger structure than the former building. Ironically, my uncle had named the house "Smiriti," a Hindi word meaning remembrance. All that was left now was the remembrance of the "remembrance." So much of human life is lived in the structure of mind, a situation commonly unappreciated by people.

While Srinagar, even in its heydays, was at best a medieval city, now it has taken the looks of an ancient city. The Dal Lake and the high mountains around it have given it a splendid backdrop for thousands of years. The city is like a poor, common looking woman, who has been dressed in a magnificent gown and a resplendent and a noble headgear, lifting her to a level of superb majesty and mesmerizing beauty. Dal Lake is serene, modest, and mystic. The mountains around it stand in a stance of frozen eternity, sentinel to the lake, their light brown luster radiating warmth and glory, standing in an obeisance to Gods. Without a visit to the lake and the several gardens fringing it the visit to the city is incomplete. It is in this spirit that I visited these places, even as I was absorbed in the tragic experience of Kashmiris in the last fourteen years.

Driving down the Boulevard toward the Moghul Gardens nothing much seemed to have changed except that more hotels and Kashmiri crafts showrooms had emerged across the road from Dal Lake. The unpaved footpath along the Boulevard remained unpaved. The lake looked forlorn. I was too focused on the general appearance of things that I paid no attention to its state of cleanliness. Even though it was sunny a thin veneer of fog covered the lake as if to defend its privacy in these flagrant times. Not many people were either on the lake or on the Boulevered. I entered Nishat Garden after twenty-six years. I found its fame of a transcendent work of art highly exaggerated. Though it is beautiful but its beauty is more due to its setting in its surroundings than due to its intrinsic merit as a garden. Its much ballyhooed terraced layout is no wonder. The garden may have looked fabulous in Moghul era and a few hundred years after that but it has not been upgraded to the present standards of gardens and that too of famous gardens. The stonework, fountains, pathways, turf, shrubs, and flowers are crying for upgrades. Without the mystic tranquility of the lake in front of them and the grand dignity of the mountains around them, Nishat and other Mughal gardens would have been very commonplace gardens.

The gardens were deserted as expected at this time of the year. The turf had turned light brown and there were no flowers left except of one variety. In their bareness the gardens revealed the structural deficiencies they have been carrying on for a long time. I could only remember the magic they cast on me and others decades ago, when the times in Kashmir were more human and I had not been exposed to some of the other gardens in the world. A garden is an expression of human heart but woven in the strands of human mind.

I visited Palace Hotel, now bought by someone from its previous owner, Oberoi. It seemed no one was staying there at the time. What made me go there was the experience of the beautiful sight of Dal Lake, Hari Parbat, and the high mountains beyond that I had in 1988. But I found some of the trees dotting the hotel property had been allowed to grow so tall as to block some of the grand view. Furthermore, the fog on the lake and clouds in the distance had changed the scene dramatically. Same could be said about the view from Shankaracharya, the place where I went next.

As the hour of my departure from the Valley drew nearer I could not help thinking of the mood of the place. It looked as if a public mourning was going on that was hiding some loss greater than what it indicated, in public's hearts and minds. Behind a facade of life-as-usual look people were unconsciously harboring a deep hurt, a deep loss, a break from an anchor. A state seemed to have evolved in their minds when there was no need to express their anguish, no desire to find out the agents which extinguished the flames in their lives. The people seemed to have crossed into a terrain where there was no hope at the moment and no need of regaining it. They were beyond Hamletian "to be or not to be" question and into acceptance of their existence as it was.

For my hosts my visit was a dramatic homecoming, coming as it was after a decade and a half, for which I was taking a security risk. They worked very hard to make it comfortable and secure and they were concerned every second that I enjoy it. Little could I tell them that I had not come to Kashmir to enjoy it–I could not do that even if I wanted to do it. The purpose of my visit to Kashmir was to feel the pain of the people living there who had gone through heart and home wrenching experiences in the last decade and a half, to see the destruction of the place I was born in, to rekindle the earliest memories of my life, to touch the hallowed land of my ancestors. I put in the hardest efforts I could command to cover my pain, to hide my sleepless nights. But in the end I realized that it was futile as my hosts understood what I was going through, through the invisible lens of the human heart, through the penetrating field of the human mind. When I said goodbye to them I felt as if I had known them since the first crack of my consciousness, as long back I had known the mountains surrounding Srinagar.

This journey to the ancient sources of my consciousness was surrealistic and sensitizing, opening ancient wounds and blurring new dreams, baring the fragility and the absurdity of human life, and bringing to focus once again in my long quest of the understanding of human life the power and drama of human condition.

As I sat in the plane ready to leave Kashmir I looked through the window at the brownish mountains afar. I was transported to the most ancient times of my life. Like an umbilical cord connected to a human baby at birth, Kashmir had breathed and sustained life in me not only at my birth, but directly and indirectly, throughout my life. Beyond my own life, small and insignificant that it is, were the lives of several millions of people dependent on it both physically and mentally. I could not help feeling sorry how Gods had given this near perfect land to Kashmiris and what they did to it. A beautiful valley was turned into a torrent of blood, a benign brotherhood between Hindu and Muslim communities was transformed into a relationship of hatred and vengeance, and a tranquility in the hearts and minds of the people was replaced with perturbation of anguish and disillusionment. I was reminded of a stanza of my poem Roots:

> *We do not know where to begin anew–*
> *Even, if we should begin at all,*
> *To resume God's work,*
> *To revive the spontaneous sparkling smiles*
> *On the faces of a thousand gloomy children,*
> *To let the lotuses grow unperturbed.*

When the plane took off the ground I felt sorrowfully that most likely I will be unable to return to Kashmir, given the ruination Kashmir was continuing to go through, given the irreversible erosion of my own life.

THE SPIRIT OF KASHMIRI PANDITS

Historical Outline From The Ancient Times Through The
Beginning Of Muslim Era

(October 13, 2002)

This brief article was a talk given in a seminar *Kashmir Day*,
organized by Kashmir Overseas Association, on October 26,
2002, at Kendall Park, New Jersey, to inform non-Kashmiri people
about the longstanding and intractable problem of Kashmir.

THE SPIRIT OF KASHMIRI PANDITS

HISTORICAL OUTLINE FROM THE ANCIENT TIMES THROUGH THE BEGINNING OF MUSLIM ERA

The American writer William Faulkner wrote," The past is never dead. It's not even past."

Our past is a powerful element of our consciousness, besides the history it provides of events that we must know to understand the world we live in and learn from. Beyond the factual mosaic of events that history attempts to be, it is the irrigator of our consciousness, whose fertility we very much depend upon for the richness of our present and future. We are living carriers of our personal and historical past. If we only learnt from history keenly the world we live in today would have been a more peaceful place.

Ancient histories of different parts of the world are wrapped in a lot of fog, particularly those in India, where history gathering art and craft was not considered a significant intellectual activity in the distant past. However Kashmir has been an exception, where good records of the times were kept, though some of them got lost.

For much of the Kashmir ancient history we depend on Nilmatpurana, the oldest extant book on Kashmir, and Pandit Kalhana's Rajatarangini. Nilmatpruana was written between 6th and 8th centuries and Rajatarangini around 1149. Later work

81

is very significant because it is the first history written in India and also because of the way it is written. Kalhana approached history in a scientific and democratic way, giving the kings and the common men the same importance while assessing the causes and significance of the events of a period under consideration. He saw the transitoriness in the material and the political power. Here was a historian with a spiritual vision of human existence. He was a Kashmiri Brahman and wrote Rajatarangini in Sanskrit verse. His book is one of the most widely used references of the ancient Indian history. After his death his work was carried on by other historians, till almost the start of the Mughal era in Kashmir.

Nilmatpurana records (in the 6th to 8th cent. period) that Kashmiris were a religious people, upholding the sacredness of the land, and leading generally a happy life. Unlike some of the other parts of India, women enjoyed considerable freedom and were looked upon with respect and honor.

The name Kashmir is found in unbroken form in ancient Hindu texts like Nilmatpurana, Ashtadhyayi, Mahabarta, the Puranas, and the Braht Samhitta over a period stretching to 2,300 years. Legend has it that King Gonanda The First of Kashmir and his son Damodra lost their lives fighting in Kureva-Pandava war of Mahabarta.

From the earliest historical times Kashmir was ruled by Hindu kings. This lasted till 1339, when Sultan Shams'd Din, popularly known as Shah Mir, an émigré from Swat (which is in the present day Pakistan),laid the foundation of the Muslim era.

The earliest known rulers of Kashmir were Gonandiyas, a Hindu dynasty which ruled for about 3,049 years. Some records were kept during this era but unfortunately they were lost. Kalhana's history is only accurate from around Karkota Dynasty onwards, before that he is supposed to have used his imagination. Following this long stretch of Hindu era was Buddhist era brought on by King Ashoka (Reign: 273-232 B.C.)

King Ashoka founded the Kashmir capital Srinagri, about three miles from the present city of Srinagar, during the time when his kingdom covered Kashmir. The city developed rapidly and became prosperous and important. He constructed a large number of temples in Kashmir. After King Ashoka's brutally Pyrrhic victory in Kalinga, Orrisa, in 261 B.C., he turned Buddhist and made Kashmir the northern center for the development and diffusion of his new religion. This was the time Buddhism flourished in Kashmiri. It is said that Buddha himself had thought that Kashmir's environment was suitable for the meditative practices of Buddhisim.

But with history's unexpected turns Buddhism receded from Kashmir for about 200 years when Ashoka's son Jaluka, separating from his father's kingdom, founded an independent state, which practiced Hinduism. It was in King Kanishka's empire that Buddhism was brought back to Kashmir and it flourished then much more than its significant success the first time around. During this time an international Buddhist council, called the 4th Council, was organized just outside the present day Srinagar, in a place called Kundalvan, which is perhaps the present-day Harwan. This council, which lasted six months, was attended by some 500 Buddhist and Hindu scholars from different countries, under the chairmanship of a Kashmiri Brahman named Vasumitra. One of the momentous results of this council was the development of Mahayana Buddhism. The council was a watershed event in the diffusion of Buddhism outside India, like to Central Asia, Tibet, China, Korea, and Japan. Renowned Buddhist missionaries Kumarrajiva, Yasa, Vimalaksha, Sangabuti, Gautamasangha, and others started from Kashmir. Also spread abroad in the process were the stories of Mahabarta and Ramayana. So it was from Kashmir that Indian culture and Sanskrit literature traveled to some of the parts of the world.

One of the bright stars in the pantheon of kings was Lalataditya (699-736). Here was an ambitious conqueror of lands, an astute administrator and statesman, and a prolific builder. In his thirty-seven years of rule he expanded Kashmir's control over Tibet, Badakhan, Punjab, and Kanuj. He created several towns, viharas, stupas, and temples, the foremost of which is the grand sun-temple Martand, built over Mattan village in Kashmir. Martand's architecture and its location are greatly admired.

Hiuen Tsiang, the reknowned Chinese monk, came to Kashmir in the seventh century via Varamullah, present-day Baramulla, and stayed for two years. He found Kashmiri scholars of high intellectual caliber.

For some two thousand years Kashmir was the prime source of Sanskrit learning and literature. It was a center for scholarly exchanges. Some of the significant scholars and poets of Sanskrit were Kashmiris: Kalhan, Bilhan, Acharya Bhamba, Udbhata, Acharya Kutanka, Mammata, Anand Vardhana, Vamana, Rudrata, Kshemendra, Abhinav Gupta, Rojanak Shitianth, and others.

One of the most significant contributions that Kashmiri Hindus have made not only to the resplendent oeuvre of Indian philosophy but to the world philosophy has been the development of Kashmir Shaivism. Shaivism is a system of thought which prescribes the attainment of *moksha* (the absolute freedom) in Shiva. Although Kashmir Shaivism and Advaita Vedanta both teach non-dualism, the non-dualism of the former is quite different from the latter's. In Kashmir Shaivism this universe is real and true but Advaita Vedanta considers it to be the other way. In Kashmir Shaivism Lord Shiva is connected with the real world through the expansion of his *shakti* and the universe is a reflection through him, as if in a mirror. Shiva and *shakti* are the same. Lord Shiva has three energies: Para, the supreme energy, Parapara, the medium or cognitive energy, and Apara, his inferior or objective energy. A human being lives in the inferior state of Shiva's energy and Kashmir Shaivism teaches how to attain Shiva's supreme energy.

We learn from the ancient Kashmiri history that fires were once lit somewhere in time in Kashmiri psyche for learning, for the pursuit of the truth of life, and for the devotion to God, which we know are still smoldering. We learn that a Kashmiri was always a lost soul in the clamorous world around him and he needed tranquility of the surroundings and a feeling of brotherhood with the fellow human beings to survive. The relationship between

Kashmir and India had been like that between two brothers, separate but belonging to the same family–a situation which has been further reinforced through the time stretching to the present.

Attached to this presentation is a chronology in the ancient Kashmiri history.

CHRONOLOGY IN ANCIENT KASHMIRI HISTORY

Sources

1.	Nilmatpurana	Written in 6th-8th Cent.(Oldest extant text on Kashmir)
2.	Kalhana's Rajatarangani	Written in 1149-50 (Kashmir history from the earliest times to 12thCent.)
3.	Jonaraja's Rajtarangani	Covers 1150-1459
4.	Jaina's Rajatarangani	Covers 1459-1486
5.	Raja Pataka	Covers 1486-1512

Chronology

~ 3677-628 B.C.	Gonandiya Dynasty (68 Kings)
273-232 B.C.	King Ashoka's rule. Develops the new city of Srinagri (see the expanded history of the city below)
~ 1-2 Cent. A.D.	4th Buddhist Council in Kundalvan, Kashmir
625-855 A.D.	Karkota Dynasty
699-736 A.D.	King Lalitaditya
7th Cent.	Hiuan Tsiang visits Kashmir

855-1003 A.D.	Utpalla Dynasty
855-883	King Avantivarman (Suyya, the great engineer, lived in this time. Syyapore, new Sopore, named after him)
950-958	King Kshemagupta
981-1003	Queen Dida's reign
1003-1089	1st Lohar Dynasty
1089-1101	King Harsha
1101-1128	2nd Lohara Dynasty
1301-1320	King Sahadeva's rule.
1320-1323	King Rainchan Shah. (Converts from Buddhism to Islam) Marries Kota Rani. First Muslim king of Kashmir
1323-1338	King Udyanadeva. Marries Kota Rani.
~1338-1339	Queen Kota Rani. Last Hindu ruler. Dies in 1339.
1339	Start Of Muslim Era
	Sultan Shams'd Din (Shah Mir rule: 1339-42)
1389-1413	Sultan Sikander (5th Sultan). Most brutal to Pandits, who left Kashmir, engendering the myth that only 11 families were left behind.
1420-1470	Zain-ul-Abidin (Budshah). The sultan most benevolent to Pandits.
1586-1751	Mughal Era
1753-1819	Pathan Era
1819-1846	Sikh Era

1846	The Treaty Of Amritsar. British sell Kashmir to Gulab Singh for 75 lakh rupees
1846-1947	Dogra Era

History Of Srinagar

The city of Srinagri was founded by King Ashoka (reign: 273-232 B.C.) at the present-day village of Pandrethan, about 3 miles of the present-day Srinagar. (Panderthan was called Purnadisthan until 14th cent.). Present-day Srinagar was founded by King Pravarsena The Second (Gonandiya Dynasaty) and used to be called Pravarpura. When the name Srinagri changed to Srinagar and replaced Pravarpura is not known.

M.Kaul 10.15.02; Rev: 11.19.11

DISILLUSIONMENT AND FAITH

The Future Of Kashmiri Pandits

(August 9, 2002)

The forced exodus of Kashmiri Pandits from their motherland of thousands of years has made them disillusioned with the institutions of the world which look after fair and human treatment of people. Yet they carry an ancient faith that has seen them through difficult times before.

DISILLUSIONMENT AND FAITH

THE FUTURE OF KASHMIRI PANDITS

When a man is robbed of his belongings, kicked out of his home, and forced to leave his land where his ancestors had lived for thousands of years, it is very hard to imagine that he will continue to have faith in the human values of his tormentors and destroyers–even of his neighbors and countrymen at large, and even that of the people around the world.

Human life is a fragile phenomenon, where the support of the physical environment and the faith in the fellow human beings is a requisite for meaningful existence.

Kashmiri Pandits, the original inhabitants of Kashmir, have been kicked and destroyed before, but never have they been so grossly brutalized, victimized, and dehumanized as this time. This destruction of Kashmiri Pandits is the most profound in their history and it will have a significant impact on their survival and happiness.

The annihilation of Pandits happened while the central government of India was watching and well aware of the dimensions of the tragedy taking place but chose to play soft with its perpetrators, Muslims, in the hope of winning the civil war in Kashmir one day. Cries of help to the people of India and beyond evoked little effective sympathy and help. Ambushed in daylight, Pandits left Kashmir Valley in pain, misery, and utter revulsion toward Muslims and disgust toward their central government–but invisibly, deep beneath their day to day consciousness, many of them harbored hopes of justice and human treatment. It took many years after being kicked out of the valley before most of them started losing faith in the mankind's mythologized human values and civilization's much vaunted democratic institutions.

Most of the KP's pass time in the dreary, pigeon-holed, futureless existence in Jammu. Thousands of men in mid-30's to mid-50's never go to work, as they have chosen to survive on government handouts given in lieu of the salary they would have earned, if they had the proper conditions to work in Kashmir. This psychological-self-annihilation is the worst price KP community is paying at the hands of the civil war. The lack of zeal, ambition, and a sense of honor to work has had devastating effect on the family happiness and the proper psychological health of KP children. Many young, professionally educated KP's have chosen to fight the mental illness and the consequent physical illness than attempt to carve a new future in places distant from Kashmir. This long immersion in slothfulness and hopelessness will cast a dark shadow on the development of the future Kashmiri culture. It will take generations before Kashmiri Pandits of Jammu and Kashmir will regain purposefulness, confidence, and cheerfulness in their lives. One has only to look at the volume of anti-depression, ulcer, and blood-pressure medications consumed by KP's in this region. Some time back there was a report that the average birth-weight of KP babies in the region was significantly deteriorating. The young KP boys and girls do not harbor big and many dreams.

One thing is clear in the present Kashmiri Pandit catastrophe, that they will never reoccupy Kashmir Valley in the same fervor, legitimacy, and bond as before. Although Kashmir will continue to remain under India, its past social and cultural atmosphere will never remerge, as it has been badly shattered. It is as if the spine of a human being has been broken in a violent collision and thereafter he can never reclaim his old poise, gait, and grace. Kashmiri Pandit's have to accept the *fait accompli* of the situation the events have thrown them into. Bleeding our hearts on the mammoth loss will not make us recover it. All the diplomacy, the political jostling and posturing going on in the world on Kashmir problem does not touch the plight of KP's. They are the side-show of the side-show in this insane and ancient drama played between Muslims and Hindus. All the intense and prolonged efforts by KP's round the world to draw attention to their injustice and pain have not produced any significant results. KP efforts have by now reached an apex, any further intensification and revision of strategy to win people to their cause will not be helpful. No energy should be expended to influence Govt. Of India, as it has its own strategy and agenda, in which KP's have a marginal weight. In such a situation KP's should give up on the hope of reclaiming Kashmir in the way it occupied it before. Kashmir can not become their home in the same way as it was before. The recent catastrophic experiences in Kashmir have alienated the dominant majority of Kashmir, Muslims, and the Hindus for a long time to come. How can a KP return to a place where his fellow KP's have been murdered, many of their houses have been burnt, by a majority community who hates them. It would not be possible to have a normal emotional and psychological life there. And an attempt to raise KP children there would be a leap into insanity. Even though Kashmir will continue to remain a part of India, it is no longer a home of KP's.

With the above perspective, it would make a lot of sense for KP organizations like Panun Kashmir and KOA to withdraw from the cause of returning KP's to Kashmir and rechannelize their energizes and financial resources to the placement of young KP's in jobs, helping in the education of the destitute children, and the creation of international networking for the sustenance of KP identity and ambition. KP's should be helped to run for local elections. They should stop beating their chests and look to future for the betterment of their children and community. There hang myths about Kashmirs that they have a sharp sense of survival and a keen mind. Although they are not accurate but Kashmiris do have some sense of survivability and some measure of mental keenness–both greatly needed in their present circumstances.

If KP's follow two things–and it seems that they eventually will–they will do quite well in future. One is to work hard and the other to not to tamper with their identity. KP's are college-education minded and this helps them greatly in these technological times. KP's are into all kinds of technological and scientific fields. One area they are not good at is private entrepreneurship; no wonder not many KP's are in that. Working hard, though not natural for Kashmiris, is accommodated by them when circumstances demand. We have to see how KP's work when they are outside Kashmir. They being *permanently* exiled from Kashmir Valley is in a way a boon for them, as their mental keenness coupled with diligence may take them to hithero unrealized achievements. Kashmiris are very comparing, that is before embarking on important things they see whether fellow Kashmiris are also doing the same. In the universal climate of hard work, engendered by cutthroat competition, KP's will follow the tide.

Identity is one of the basic structures of human psychology, any attempt to modify it is risking a lot. KP's have to keep nourishing their identity (but not necessarily continue with some bad things of the old culture). This should take form of the community cultural clubs, international gatherings on history, art, and literature of Kashmir, etc. The internet revolution is obviously a bonanza to the uprooted communities like KP's. As long as KP's consider themselves first as Kashmiris and then as Indians, they have a better chance of retaining their Kashmiri identity. Having been rendered refugees in the country of their citizenship, they can not do any better. Like Jews we have been rendered rootless and like them we will become cosmopolitan and mixable with other communities, but without losing our identity. Like them our history will become our destiny. Our greatest pitfall will be if we try to become Americans or British or French, etc. We have to live through our Kashmiri identity to live in peace, dignity, and happiness.

Contrary to popular opinion there will be people living in the world a hundred years from now, who will not only call themselves KP's but be KP's–though different from us, to account for the passage of time and the change of circumstances. They may not be speaking Kashmiri, same way as many Europeans in U.S.A. do not speak their ancestral languages. The whole world is changing in that the ethnicity of its groups is diluting as global village metaphor is hitting the ground. We will be a colored element in a vast kaleidoscope. From the high pedestal of Kashmiri Brahmin we have to descend gracefully to become a mere flower in a widespread garden. History has taught us that ethnicity does not disappear, though it may change its appearance. Also, Kashmiris, in spite of complex relationships they often have with each other, do not mix well with other ethnic groups. Networking will remain the backbone of the Kashmiri psychological survival. They are vastly more inclined to the psychological condition of "being," rather than of "becoming." Kashmiris seek their kind, even the one's they would have reservations about mixing with back home, outside Kashmir, in foreign lands, wherever they are spread thin. Kashmiris, history has shown us, have resistance to change. Kashmiris will survive ethnically as Italians, Irish, Spanish, and other groups have. Identity and survival are in their genes.

Moving out of Jammu and Kashmir as refugees and restarting their lives has been traumatic for more than one reason. A refugee's resettlement is expectedly fraught with anguish and perspiration, but in a KP's case the added dimension of heart-break came from our central government's apathy and neglect–which has been so bad that it seems it was calculatedly done. Add to it the lack of sympathy and help from the non-Kashmiri Indian (the significant help from Bal Thackeray and others has only been a drop in the ocean), which has hurt the KP pride very badly. There are only about 800,000 KP's round the world, but they have a high estimation of their legacy, character, and personality, and, therefore, they are understandably a proud people. Indian people are battling a universe of problems, the plight of KP's is only a small air current in a hurricane they live in. KP's can not find proper sympathy, help, and opportunity to transplant themselves in India outside Jammu and Kashmmir after their destruction and desecration in land of their ancestors. They have to seek refuge outside India, if possible.

United States is a special place in the world at this time in history. It is not only the biggest nation of the immigrants but also a champion of democracy and is economically the strongest engine in the world. No wonder it has been a magnet to the world's disaffected, disfranchised, and deprived. KP's have a logical place to attempt to emigrate to in their circumstances. There are some one thousand KP families in U.S. eager to help them. Given the ethnic multiplicity and tolerance in the country, U.S. is the most suitable place for KP diaspora to land at. Even though it is far from Kashmir, it is the most suitable garden in which the fragile KP plant has the best chance of transplantation. We can try, at a larger scale, to influence U.S. Govt. to give us refugee treatment in giving us land and financial support. This simple idea has unfortunately not been give a chance. Better than living in India, U.S.A. would best serve the long-time goals of many KP's.

Disillusionment is the present state of mind of the KP refugee, we could not expect any different from his circumstances. For thousands of years he clung to his mother Kashmir but now time has come for him to take a radical step, a step to make a clean break from the past illusions, and at last tread on the ground leading to liberation. We have been a target of religious hatred, a political bargaining chip, and a peripherally insignificant minority for a long time but now fate gives us a chance to escape the turmoil and a torture of hundreds of years–a chance we can not lose, an opportunity we can not spoil. Future beckons us. Faith has been simplistically described as belief without reason. But we need not abandon reason in having faith that KP's will transcend the present impasse and emerge as a more successful and happier community than before. All we have to do is work hard, retain our identity, and try to leave India. The subconscious religiosity of KP's, their non-conformist inclinations, their strong love for nature, and their disinclination toward a personal god are all ingredients for a people who can transplant themselves to different places and cultures in the world.

THE FUTURE OF KASHMIR

(May 9, 1998)

An assessment of the Kashmir Problem nine years after the present civil war.

THE FUTURE OF KASHMIR

We stand today at a strange moment in Kashmir's ongoing drama. While we are not yet over with its recent tragic past, we are haunted by the questions of why did what happened there happen, and by what will happen there in the next five, ten years. Needless to say that the two questions are connected.

The tragedy of Kashmir is the tragedy of human nature; its blindness, its greed, its ignorance, its sheer stupidity.

Kashmiri Muslims did not find in 1947 their religious tug strong enough to have raised their hand for throwing their lot with Pakistan; but yet by 1989 they took a suicidal leap to do that, even though in the interim they lead a more prosperous time in their history than ever before. Strange are the ways of human psychology. Why would any people join one of the most rickety economies in the world, and one of its most politically benighted nations. While religion is the most imaginative and sublime of man's creations, but it has proven to be also the most stupefying and blinding.

What will happen to Kashmir in the next ten years? We do not have to depend upon the politicians on both sides of the divide to enhance the conditions for human living, the human instinct to survive and live peacefully has regained enough momentum in Kashmir to proceed its course in spite of their selfishness, greed, and narrow-mindedness. Humanness overcomes politics, as survival precedes faith. Kashmiris are getting out of the grip of terrorism and the instincts of life are gaining strength. The last eight years of their lives have to be reckoned as their brush with insanity. As individuals go through mental crisis, communities, even nations, go through mental crisis. Kashmiri Muslims thought their bliss was to be integrated with the Islamic State Of Pakistan, but the hard geopolitical realities would not allow that to happen. Having lost their homes and hearth, brothers and neighbors, their peace of mind and image, they have realized that they were better off in all aspects of life before their rendezvous with the fantasy of establishing a religious state. Do not reason with a people whose fantasies have just been shattered. Not only is this a period of economic, political, and infrastructure repair in Kashmir, but also of the minds of the people who risked almost everything they had to be the devil's advocate.

Indian Government's governing of Kashmir has been as colossal a failure as any had by a government. Much more than the failure of the nuts and bolts of the governing, it has been a failure to grasp the essence of the Kashmir and India integration. You can not develop and strengthen a relationship by money and guns. You can not isolate a people and still expect them to be a part of you. Human relationship, whether at individual or community level, is a dynamic condition. Leaving Kashmiris in a political, social, and economic freezer, their alienation turned to seeking security and strength in religious identification.

Much castigated nowadays is the legal and political condition called Article 370, which ties India with Kashmir. It is particularly the younger generation who is much troubled with it and angry with the Indian leaders who accepted it at the infancy of the Indo-Kashmir integration. They do not understand that Kashmir was not like any other state who had thrown its lot with India; it had remained a separate political and historical entity for hundreds of years. Sheikh Abdullah chose to integrate Kashmir with India over Pakistan, but he wanted to maintain Kashmir's historical autonomy. India could not have done anything about it; it had either to accept this condition or lose Kashmir. But much water has gone down Jehlum since the condition was consummated; time is overdue for its revocation. If India had understood the integration with Kashmir rightly, conditions of the revocation would have reached much earlier. Of course, it cannot be done right now in the present seething political climate of Kashmir and under the glare of the international headlights, but three to four years from now it would be feasible.

Even Indian Government will have to learn from its mistakes. Kashmir has to be treated like another state of India, otherwise another civil war will be planted there by its arch enemy and neighbor, Pakistan. The son-in-law treatment of Kashmiris has gone in a long way to make them irresponsible citizens. India has to remove all its latent guilt of thinking that it is occupying Kashmir against the will of its inhabitants; the fact is that in 1949 Kashmiris made a willful decision to join India; and they profited immensely from that. When non-Kashmiri Indians can buy property in Kashmir, when Indian businesses can control employment there, the perspective of Kashmiris will be forced to change. When government subsidies are lifted and people have to compete for a living, survival instinct will overwhelm religious fantasies. Let any Kashmiri wanting to emigrate to Pakistan be allowed to do so, but only on no-return basis.

Certainly, the biggest problem for India in the Kashmir situation has not been its inhabitants, but the ever evil-designing Pakistan. How many nations in the world would have reacted passively as India did, when Pakistan was destabilizing it simultaneously in two places, Punjab and Kashmir. Can you imagine Germany, France, Great Britain, U.S. practically doing nothing while its militarily comparable neighbors are undermining their security. If we cannot make Pakistan realize the consequences of its weakening of India's integrity, then we might as well hand over Kashmir to them, sparing the blood of many innocents and the grief of the survivors.

Also if we can not seal the very porous border between Kashmir and Pakistan due to the weaknesses of our military personnel, then we are again better–off gifting Kashmir to Pakistan.

A gain has accrued in the tragic turmoil of Kashmir, that of the shattering of Kashmiri Muslims' fantasy that if they raised their hands for Pakistan, it would go to the great lengths to secure their integration with itself. Pakistan demonstrated quite unequivocally that it could only do so much for its beloved Kashmiris. Also the unrestrained violence of the militants has left a large number of Muslims cold. In two to three years Kashmir will grow into a stable and livable place, with the unshakable attendant stigma of destruction, violence, and tragedy hanging over the heads of its inhabitants for a long time to come. The culture of the place has been permanently altered. Many children will grow with aberrant psyches. The shadow of distrust between Hindu and Muslim communities will endure for several decades.

The above picture of the future of Kashmir is idealized. Actually Indian government will not be able to shake off all its inhibitions, apprehensions, and inertia about Kashmir rapidly; Kashmiri Muslims will not totally forget their inflamed religious passion for the vision of an Islamic state of Kashmir; Pakistan can not, both for its political and psychological reasons, cut itself off from Kashmir. Kashmir's return to normalcy will continue, but it will be laced with many setbacks, violent opposition, sabotages, and false-steps. The drama of the Kashmiri stupidity, Indian incompetence, and Pakistani greed will continue for a while, impeding the progress in Kashmir. In the long run Kashmir will regain its equilibrium and humanity; some of the illusions of all the major parties involved will be shattered.

Kashmiri Pandits, the tragic victims of the Kashmir war, will continue to remain refugees in their land for a while. The militants see their return as ultimate defeat of their objective in Kashmir. Therefore, they will continue to indulge in activities like the massacres in Wandhama and Sangrampura to discourage the Pandit resettlement. Pandits will never inhabit Kashmir in the same way as they did before.

KASHMIRI REFUGEES' SETTLEMENT IN U.S.

(June 27,1997)

This writing is based on a debate on Internet over settling Kashmiri Pandit refugees is U.S.

KASHMIRI REFUGEES' SETTLEMENT IN U.S.

Kasmiri refugees' settlement in US has produced intense and argumentative debate, which is understandable in light of the topic's emotional import.

Perhaps, every Kashmiri has a theory on how to help the refugees; although, they may be categorized into just a few, as only small differences separate many of them from each other.

The idea of the resettlement of the refugees to US is a good one; the only problem I have posed is how feasible it is.

Some of the participants (Subash Kak, Anupam Kaul) in the debate are confident that it is feasible; but I have doubts based on the personality of KP's and the world geopolitical situation. The examples of other people who have successfully transplanted themselves as political refugees are not applicable to KP refugees, because of their entirely different circumstances.

It does not mean that those who strongly feel about the issue should not try its realization. The first step of such a project is to distribute a questionnaire in the camps. Certainly, that can not be organized through Panun Kashmir, because they are selling the dream of an island-Kashmir in the geographical Kashmir; which is directly contradictory to the KP emigration to a foreign land.

It will take about a year to find the feasibility of such an idea. A group of people can devote themselves to it.

Following answers are specifically for the questions asked by Susheel Jalali Sahib:

When I wrote that history is replete with human groups overcoming unfair treatment, I did not mean that it can be done in a short time. Eight years of the KP struggle is very small compared to many similar struggles. In the long run, I am sure, KP's will find a strong footing in Kashmir.(There are many reasons behind my thinking; one of them being the utter preponderance of the Hindus over the Muslims in India)

Panun Kashmir by putting an unrealistic goal of acquiring an island-Kashmir in the geographic Kashmir has lost its credibility with KP's, non-Kashmiri Indians, GOI, and other KP-sympathizing countries. It does not appear to be a grassroots organization. It is a propaganda organization. We need some propagandists in our fight, but we also need good communicators, organizers, protesters, and skilled "lobbyists." It has not been an effective instrument in getting us some attention and help.(And if it has not succeeded in eight years, it is time to think of an alternative.)

By "winning" is meant gaining our full Indian citizenship. (Right now we are like 'foreigners' in our own country). Also, by "winning' is meant that we are able to return to Kashmir and be treated like human beings by our government.

INSANITY AND INSENSITIVITY

Reflections On Kashmir Problem

(June 7, 1997)

This article looks into the conditions of insanity and insensitivity that have caused and maintained the Kashmir Problem.

INSANITY AND INSENSITIVITY

REFLECTIONS ON KASHMIR PROBLEM

After a magnificent victory of big dimensions one does not, generally, stop to think the underlying causes behind it; but in the aftermath of a mammoth failure one is compelled to ponder its avoidability.

The irenic and languorous people of Kashmir lie today physically impoverished, mentally rattled, economically devastated, and politically dead. The physical grandeur of Kashmir lies in shambles. Heavy layers of gloom surround the moribund existence of its people, who are spiritually exhausted, staring blankly at the future.

The Kashmiri children will bear the greatest damage of all the people in the conflagration. Their psyches will grow aberrated, robbing them of full and healthy lives. The culture of the place has suffered a violent wound, which will take decades to heal, leaving forever an excruciating stigma.

What caused this calm and care-free people living in majestically beautiful and idyllic surroundings, riding along turbulence-free history, to explode so violently?

When the greatest Kashmiri leader Sheikh Mohammad Abdullah was asked why he decided to throw his political lot with Hindu India rather than with Muslim Pakistan, he answered that he did so only because he thought his people would prosper more. He was right on the mark. In the period between 1947, the year modern Kashmir was created, and 1989, the year when the ongoing civil war became a force to reckon with, Kashmiris experienced a huge economic upliftment, unprecedented in their history. They were the unquestioned masters of their land politically, culturally, and in the practice of their religion.

What laid the seeds of their insanity was their psychologically insecure identity. They never felt they were part of India, in spite of living grandly on its resources. This irrationality of apartness from India, maturing into alienation, became the bedrock of the political divide.

Why would anyone join an economically crippled and politically benighted Pakistan, which since its inception fifty years ago has played a havoc with its existence? It is a nation without a reliable structure of government; unrelentingly under the evil control of its military ;without the tangible will for political change in its much frustrated, tired, and resigned people. It is one of the most exploited, confused, and backward nations in the world. It draws sustenance from the efforts it expends on destabilizing its neighbor. It is a nation without a program and without an awareness of the severity of its problems.

When Pakistan is not able to take care of itself, how can it take care of the added burden of Kashmir, which has no significant economic resources. But acquiring Kashmir is not a tangible plan for Pakistan, but a blinder set up by its politicians to divert its people's attention at their colossal problems, a tranquilizer provided to make them forget its bleak record and unpromising future. Pakistani leaders know that Kashmir cannot be wrested from India, but they want their people to have the illusion to the contrary. There have been few nations in the history of the world in which politicians squandered so much national wealth and energy, and fooled its people so long, for so little.

A Kashmiri would remain a much stigmatized second-class citizen in the expanded nation of Pakistan and Kashmir. From the very outset the new province of Kashmir would be a seething cauldron of political intrigue and unrest. Its former economic security will pulverize into paralysis and panic. Kashmiris will beat their chests for their catastrophic blindness.

This drama of the insane hunter and the blinded prey is tragic, traumatic, and devastating.

An independent nation of Kashmir is a geopolitical impossibility at this time.

Behind the glossy but tragic drama of the hunter and the hunted lies the egregious devastation of the original inhabitants of Kashmir, the Kashmiri Pandits. Some three thousand Pandits were expended casually, just to give color and excitement to the cause of the Islamization of Kashmir. Another three hundred thousand were kicked out of their homes by the vicious fear and the scorching threats unleashed by the militants against them. Rendered refugees in their own land, they are leading miserable and wasted lives in camps. Their children are growing without proper nutrition, education, and future.

These unmourned victims of the Kashmir crisis have even been forsaken by their own government. Never has a government knowingly neglected the victims of a civil war raging in its country to appease the criminal group responsible for it as much as in the Kashmir war. In fact, Govt. Of India's strategy is to maintain the brotherly relationship with the militant-sympathizers, in the hope that one day they will come around, as it happened in the Nagaland crisis. The government has let the Kashmiri Pandits wither away, to keep the Kashmiri Muslims less critical of them.

What has the rest of the world done for the Pandits? There have been no international relief measures taken for them. In fact, most of the world does know much about their plight. A few thousand deaths and a few hundred thousand refugees do not excite the humanity very much these days. The devastation has to be much larger to occupy the world news headlines.(Bosnia is supposed to have completely eclipsed Kashmir).

Pakistan's proxy war in Kashmir has not elicited much criticism in the world. People have turned their heads away in the West from the vicious Pakistani invasion, because it has happened in the East, and also because Pakistan had been a friend of the West for a long time. Morality at the international level is a matter of region, race, and convenience.

Throughout the history there have been some wars and upheavals based on the insanity of the participants rather than on the territorial and economic reasons. The war in Kashmir is a splendid example of this genre. The mankind's collective will is still so diffused, light in ambition, and unsure of its morality, that it cannot be counted on saving a part of it at this time.

EMPEROR'S CLOTHES

(December 1994)

This article is about the 19 U.S. Congressmen's letter to President Clinton to declare Pakistan as a terrorist nation.

EMPEROR'S CLOTHES

Courage is to raise one's head in a crowd, unmindful of its possible disapproval or condemnation of what one stands for. Such defiance of possible odds against one's position comes not from blindness of the situation one is involved in, nor from the combative zeal one is possessed with to fight the critics of one's cause (although that is needed in situations of strong and unpopular convictions), but the strength comes from the belief in the principles behind the cause one stands for.

Nineteen U.S. Congressmen stand for the principle of stopping the state-run international terrorism, which is operating devastatingly all over the world from its base in Pakistan. They no longer want to remain under the stupor of diplomatic niceties and moral infantilism, they want to call the Emperor without clothes to be what it is–naked.

Pakistan is a country which never grew up. From three decades of military dictatorship to crass opportunism of its politicians, it is the story full of betrayal, greed, and blindness. It is one of the most backward countries in the world. In recent era it has become one of the bastions of international terrorism, to grease the pockets of some and soak the religious fervor of others. The rape of Kashmir is a case in point. This beautiful and tranquil region of India has been held as a bounty for decades in front of Pakistanis, since its inception as a state, by its political leaders to divert their attention from their mammoth problems of hunger, poverty, disease, and disorder. Pakistani engineered and financed terrorism has devastated Kashmir economically, politically, and culturally. Also, it has rendered 300.000 of its Hindus refugees in their own country.

Terrorism has become like natural disasters: it is unpredictable, cataclysmic, and unstoppable. But it does not have to be like that. It is created by human beings and it can be stopped by human beings. All we need is a conscience to speak about it.

Last 10 years have witnessed the proliferation of terrorism around the world. With the burgeoning and the ripening of the world-wide democratic movement, it is perplexing to see how an anti-democratic human behavior has mushroomed into a powerful force to reckon with. The roots of this aberrant human behavior lie not in the nature of the democracy surrounding it, but in the reckless expression of its sister-culture, individualism. Unfettered individualism has, at times, led to beliefs and actions contrary to common human interest. Turning the head away from the rising epidemic of terrorism has sustained its growth and power.

We cannot sit idly, harboring misgivings, seething with anger and repugnance, and let the sword of terrorism inflict a thousand wounds on mankind.

Most of the terrorism has roots in politics and religion. For the civilized countries to sit on the sidelines, on the grounds of the decency of non-interference in the affairs of other countries, is a dereliction of duty, a denial of conscience, an invitation to disaster. The world is now an interconnected mosaic, a political catastrophe in one part quickly travels to other parts. One has to be judgmental about certain basic human values like democracy and peace, cultural tolerance and human rights. We have to protect these basic conditions of human existence, wherever they are in jeopardy. A cancer in one part of body may travel to others.

We applaud and salute the courage of the nineteen Congressmen who have written to President Clinton to declare Pakistan a terrorist country. They have not turned their heads away from one of the bastions of world terrorism, but they want their country and the others to do something about it. We cannot let the progress of civilization be impeded by the insane behavior of some countries.

Congratulations Congressmen. History will make your action unforgettable and mankind will be ever grateful to you.

Rally To Protest Pakistan's Presentation Of Kashmir Case In U.N.

(October 4, 1994)

A rally to protest Pakistani government's presentation of its case on Kashmir to United Nations was staged in front of it. It comprised of Kashmiri Pandits and other Indians.

RALLY TO PROTEST PAKISTAN'S PRESENTATION OF KASHMIR CASE IN U.N.

To launch a strong and stirring protest to Pakistan's continuing campaign of death, destruction, and dismemberment in Kashmir to acquire it, we want the Kashmiri community in U.S. and Canada to participate in a rally in front of U.N. Headquarters in N.Y. City, on 10-4-94, when Pakistan presents its Kashmir case to the U.N. General Assembly.

The massacre of eight thousand people in Kashmir has wrecked havoc in the Kashmiri life and psyche. Three-hundred thousand members of the innocent Hindu minority were forced to flee from their homes to find refuge outside the Valley. Many of their abandoned homes were later burned down by the militants and their supporters. Most of the refugees are living in sub-human conditions, on $30 per month Government provided dole, without occupation, without proper education for their children, and without hope of return to decent life, dignity, or Kashmir.

The Kashmir crisis has reached a point where it is possible that we may lose it in not so distant future. This calamity will bring unspeakable pain to the Kashmiris worldwide, dismember India of an ancient and significant part, trigger the withering away of a finely tapestried culture, and turn the decades old echo of historical tranquility in the region into a wider war and chaos.

We want the Kashmiri community to demonstrate in the protest rally that they will fight the Pakistani brutal aggression and tear apart the lies it is going to speak in the U.N. and they will tell the world the truth of Pakistan's inhuman, sordid, evil-designs in Kashmir,

Your presence is required to send the message to U.N. loud and clear that truth and justice will prevail over lies and evil. The enemies of Kashmir have held the ground for a long time, but now they are running out of tricks and time. They have aroused the wrath of a patient people and challenged their will. If Kashmir dies can we live, and if we live can we let Kashmir die.

Rally Data:

Date: 10-4-94, Time: 12:00 to 3:00 P.M., Location : U.N. Headquarters, N.Y. City

THE INDOMITABLE KASHMIRI SPIRIT

Will Not Give In To Barbarism, Greed, and Lies

(October 4, 1994)

A speech written for a rally to protest Pakistan's presentation of its case for the Kashmir Problem in United Nations.

THE INDOMITABLE
KASHMIRI SPIRIT

WILL NOT GIVE IN TO BARBARISM, GREED, AND LIES

Brothers and sisters:

I speak here today on behalf of the women of Kashinir who have lost their sons and husbands; neighbors and friends; who have lost their homes and neighborhoods; and who have lost their peace of mind and sanity.

The enchantingly beautiful land of Kashmir and its intrinsically tranquil and peaceful people have been systematically and cataclysmically destroyed by the blind greed and barbarism of its neighbor, Pakistan. It will take decades to restore what Kashnür has lost, both materially and spiritually.

We want the Pakistani delegation to the United Nations to realize that the capture of Kashmir will not improve their country's terribly impoverished economical, political, and morale conditions. When the Pakistan Government can not take care of its own country, how can it take care of Kashinir. It has to stand on its two legs and improve the conditions of its people, and not divert their attention from the dire problems they are facing by dangling the bounty of Kashmir in front of them. Annexation of parts of other countries on the basis of religion is extreme backwardness.

We want the Pakistani delegates to hear the message loud and clear that Kashmir belongs to Kashmlris and they have chosen to be with India in 1947, after Pakistan tried and failed to capture the whole of Kashmir. If Pakistan has any moral caliber, it must free the part of Kashmir it has been occupying forcibly for the last forty-five years.

The mothers, daughters, and sisters of Kashmir want Pakistan to know that each day it brutalizes Kahmiris, each time it mutilates Kashmir, it earns the hatred of Kashmiris and the civilized people of the world, and it strengthens their resolve to fight the enemy.

Guns will not silence our voice and lies will not change our mind. The spirit of truth is awake and the concern for justice is at work.

Long live Kashmir, long live its mothers, daughters, and sisters.

REFLECTIONS ON KASHMIR PROBLEM

(June 23, 1994)

Another analysis of the Kashmir Problem.

REFLECTIONS ON
KASHMIR PROBLEM

When we look at Kashmir problem we are appalled by the enormousness of the devastation to its physical, economic, cultural, political, and its peoples' psychological infrastructure. Its famed beauty lies in shambles and its noted tranquil and intelligent people have been transformed into fanatic, destructive tyrants.

What has wrought this havoc, who has planted these demons?

The problem of Kashmir emanates from the crisis of soul of its Muslim inhabitants. Muslims round the world are in a psychological turmoil. The conflict between the pristine and secure world of Islam and the scientific humanism with the accent on unvarnished realism of modern life has made them enemies of science, democracy and common pleasures of life. The worldwide Islamic fundamentalist revolution was not expected to miss Kashmir, even though its geopolitical situation seemed to lull some people in thinking so. Furthermore, Kashmiri Muslims' special burden of non-identification with India added to the chemistry of trauma. If Pakistan would have not been so eager to exploit India's week leadership at the time, Kashmir would have continued to remain a seething but secure bomb. The Pakistani intrigue lifted Kashmiri Muslims' vague but restrained unhappiness by psychological exploitation, death threat, and massive infusion of arms and money to a level of civil war.

Pakistan has longed and hungered for Kashmir since its creation. Some of its political leaders and artists dreamed of attaching the hauntingly beautiful Eden as the prime jewel to the hard won Islamic crown–Pakistan. More than the figment of imagination, Kashmir has proved to be an indispensable political tool used by politicians ever since Pakistan's inception to divert the attention of its people from the urgent problems of hunger and chaos. In a non-secular state the danger to the religious survival, in this case a fictitious one created in the form of Kashmir's relationship with India, is paramount. So Pakistan cannot let go of Kashmir, as long as the present political climate continues. For an expenditure of just a few *crores* of rupees a year it is able to provide political glue to its fractious population and destabilize its arch-enemy–India.

Since independent nation of Kashmir is a geopolitical impossibility, its merger with Pakistan is the best Kashmiri Muslims can hope for in their quest for an Islamic state. But the Pakistani citizenship will only be of second class. Furthermore, the economic and political crises of Pakistan will significantly downgrade Kashmirs' lifestyle. This material and psychological suicide by Kashmiri Muslims is a manifestation of the crisis of soul they are undergoing.

To the traumatized, the concerned, and the curious people with different involvements with the Kashmir problem, Government Of India's Kashmir strategy is a puzzle. Why would it let the turmoil stretch so long when the militant's military power is insignificant compared to its own. By various estimates there are no more than 6000 militants in Kashmir at this time. Any other government in place of the Indian government, having the military superiority and the favorable sovereignty status it has, would have crushed the rebels a long time ago–particularly when their sponsor, a neighbor country, has already tried to destabilize it in another region. But we know India's problems are that of guilt, incompetence, and weak leadership. It is unthinkable that a Nehru or a Gandhi (Indira) would have let the situation mess up so much.

Government Of India, with the pride of having solved problems similar to Kashmir earlier in Nagaland and Punjab under its chest, believes four years of turmoil is still too little struggle with its enemies to process into sucess. It has chosen low-level armed confrontation with militants and a protective relationship with its sympathizers as against full military engagement and carrot and stick approach. The chosen strategy has been perfected in Nagaland and Punjab and gives the semblance of an inter-group estrangement being brought under control by police forces rather than letting the situation be exposed by the use of full military forces as a civil war with international dimensions that it is. This slow processing of the problem toward the ultimate goal of the rehabilitation of law and order and political life is Government's bedrock strategy. That is why it gives monthly dole of support to boatmen, taxi drivers, shopkeepers, and sells the fruit of orchid owners outside Kashmir. The 'big brother' thinks that when the 'family feud' is over the 'little brother' will realize the former's vision, temperance, and benevolence. So time in the Kashmir problem solution is of little priority to the Government.

The brutality of the Government forces in Kashmir is the reflection of the misdirection and the inaptitude of its operations and not New Delhi's strategy. Guerilla wars are very difficult to fight to begin with and if to that is added India's legendary incompetence, the bizarreness of the outcome in the Kashmir confrontation is not a surprise. We are reminded of the mess the U.S. troops created in Vietnam. At any rate, the needless deaths are uncondonable.

This strategy is inhuman and absurd. By letting the daily doses of death, devastation, and chaos go on, the Govt. is indirectly torturing and tormenting innocent people who want nothing more than normal services of medical care and street security, and ambiance of peaceful existence.

Kashmir problem can only be resolved by the use of full Indian military power. No international mediation will work. Nor will Pakistan ever agree to division of Kashmir. There is no other significant compromise it can make. Already deluded and brainwashed, Kashmiri Muslims will be further alienated the more the present standoff is stretched.

The proposal of the rising Kashmiri Pundit organization, Panun Kashmir, to carve a piece of land out of the present boundaries of Kashmir for the Pandits is impractical. It only has a propaganda value at the cost of the seriousness of the organization to solve the Kashmir problem. There is no other way but for Hindus and Muslims to live together peacefully in Kashmir as they have done for centuries. But this obvious thing has been lost to the famed Kashmiri survival instinct at this time in their history. They say when misfortune strikes a man the biggest causality is his mind.

Should India give away Kashmir to its Muslim inhabitants (which in practical terms means giving it to Pakistan) just because they want to live in an Islamic state–even though it means their living in a politically and economically impoverished state. In this day and age to change a secular state to a religious one would be a breach of principle, a step backward in darkness. We are already burdened with the existing religious states about which we can do nothing.

THE CAUSE FOR PEACE
IN KASHMIR LIVES ON

(March 18, 1994)

A speech delivered to a gathering of Kashmiri Pandits, other Indians, Indian Consular General in New York, and media, at the residence of Dr. Bal Krishen Koul, at West Caldwell, New Jersey, to draw attention to the plight of Kashmiri Pandit refugees engendered by the ongoing civil war in Kashmir. It was organized by Kashmir Solidarity U.S.A.

THE CAUSE FOR PEACE IN KASHMIR LIVES ON

We gather here today with a common concern, pain, and hope for the victims of the Kashmir catastrophe–regardless of their religious affiliations.

The massacre of eight thousand people has wrecked a havoc in the Kashmiri life and psyche, which will not be healed in decades to come. As if this devastation was not enough, three hundred thousand people were forced to flee from their homes to find refuge outside the Valley. Many of their abandoned homes were later burned down by the militants' supporters. Most of the refugees are living in camps, in subhuman conditions, on $30 a month government provided dole per former earning family member, in high temperatures they are unused to, without occupation, and without hope of return to decent life and dignity. The plight of their older family members, the education of their young ones, the advancing age of their unmarried daughters-these are the worries that consume their energies and have wiped off smiles from their faces.

The Kashmir crisis has reached a point where it is possible that we may lose it in not so distant future. This calamity will bring unspeakable pain to the Kashmiris worldwide, dismember India of an ancient and a significant part, trigger the withering away of a finely tapestried culture, and turn the decades old echo of historical tranquility in the region into a wider war and chaos.

This evening we will share our sorrow over the tragedy that has engulfed our people and land. We will also fortify our resolve to defeat the well orchestrated terrorist campaign masterminded by our arch enemy Pakistan-which has hungered to enclave Kashmir for long to help its internal political problems. This evening we will also reenergize our hopes that civilized world will prevail over religious fanatics and inhuman politicians.

Sensitive and thoughtful Kashmiris world over want the present upheaval in their homeland to end to let the Muslims, Hindus, Sikhs, and others return to the land of their birth, to their homes, and live in harmony and peace with each other, like they did for decades-which blends with the natural beauty and tranquility of the place. The turmoil in Kashmir is foreign to its personality.

The distinguished guests amidst us, Hon. H.M. Ansari and Consul General Wakankar, have to help us realize our goals. They have to be our links with the Central Govt. in New Delhi. They have to keep us informed about the developments in Kashmir. They have to convey our concern for the refugees to the Center. We want the Center to know that it has fallen very short in helping the refugees of the war. Kashmiris have served their nation well but at this hour of their need they want their nation to help them. Govt. and the Kashmiri community here should combine resources and experience for the furtherance of the Kashmir cause.

Today's function has been organized under the sponsorship of Kashmir Solidarity U.S.A., which under the leadership of Mr. Surinder Zutshi has endeavored to bring the attention of American media, people, and political leadership to the Kashmir tragedy. Last year, the organization held a seminar on the Kashmir problem in N.Y. City with Congressman Robert Torricelli as the main speaker, who affirmed the irrevocability of Kashmir's alliance with India. Three of its members visited the refugee camps to assess the situation first-hand and later met some officials in the U.S. State Dept. to amplify their awareness of the problems, Furthermore, it organized a rally at Capitol, in Washington D.C.

to draw attention of the lawmakers and media to the suffering of the refugees.

But Kashmir Solidarity U.S.A. is only one of the several organizations devoted to the Kashmir cause. Notably two of them, Kashmir Overseas Association and Indo American Kashmir Forum have also done excellent work in this area. Plurality of organizations is not a problem. It is just a manifestation of regional alliances differing in styles and slogans, and leadership personality variations. Their cause is the same and their goals are the same. If the situation were to demand a confluence of these organizations, we are confident that they will shed their skins off and march together to the same tune. There are also individual contributors to the cause many of whom prefer to remain anonymous, without desire for recognition and deliberately keeping out of spotlight.

The enemies of Kashmir have held the ground for a long time but now they are running out of tricks and time. They have aroused the wrath of a patient people and they have challenged our will. If Kashmir dies, can we live? And if we live, can we let Kashmir die?

THE SUICIDE IN KASHMIR

(May 1993)

An exploration of the Kashmiri Muslims' mind which has lead to the crisis called Kashmir Problem.

THE SUICIDE IN KASHMIR

Human tragedies are caused, generally, by forces outside the victim's mind. Self-inflicted devastation on a mass scale is uncommon. That is why understanding the madness reigning over Kashmir is intriguing.

A revolution is a statement in action against an existing system which is contrary to a significant principle of human existence or value. Kashmiri Muslims are fighting to convert their Indian citizenship to a Pakistani one. Independent Kashmir is a hallucination harbored by the most feeble minded of the separatist zealots. Any declared Kashmir independence will not survive a week because Pakistan will trample it and replace it with its flag. Purity of motivation is not an issue in understanding the bizarre behavior of Kashmiri Muslims, it is the worthwhileness of the price they are paying to capture the prize they are after that is questionable. Once enjoined with co-religionists, Muslims will be humiliated and relegated to a second-class citizenship. The abandonment of the present secure and unhampered relationship with India to become an unequal and fragile part of an impoverished, undemocratic, and benighted Pakistan is an eclipse of mind and a stifling of the instinct to survive.

In an unthinking sweep of destruction, Kashmiri Muslims are erasing the centuries old finely tapestried culture and turning the decades old echo of historical tranquility into a nightmare of death and isolation, cruelly breaking the long bonds with the dominant inhabitants of the subcontinent, Hindus, and subjecting themselves to economic and political catastrophe. All this they are doing for the imagined bliss of cohabiting only with the fellow co-religionists. Giving up all the present life sustaining security and secular ideals for this fantasy is an obliteration of reality into extreme, a suicide without a redeeming cause.

Muslims have lived in Kashmir since the fourteenth century, before that it was predominantly a Hindu inhabited and ruled place, in fact, one of the resplendent centers of Hindu culture. Most of the Muslims in Kashmir converted from Hinduism. Frictions between the two, though ever present, have at times climaxed to murder, savage behavior, and most primitive hatred. But in the last several decades the two had learned to live with each other. Sharply different though Hinduism and Islam are from each other, the almost common culture, the common language, the shared history, and the instinct to survive had woven the until-now durable web of co-existence between the two.

Continuing the momentum of coexistence with Hindus, the Muslims did not try for separation at the most opportune time, the Indian partition in 1947. During the integration of the Indian states and kingdoms in 1947, Sardar Patel and V.P. Menon, the architects of the project, did not try to capture Kashmir in the net, because of its odd Muslim majority and an independent and arrogant king, Han Singh. And, also, because their hands were full working on what was within their grasp. Not only did not Muslims try to part with India, but they did not express any feelings contrary to this. There were no debates, meetings, or protests to lay down the separation-with-India line of thinking. In fact, their greatest leader, Sheikh Muhammad Abdullah, assiduously worked to weld the Indian Kashmiri divide. That Kashmir Muslims offered themselves voluntarily and freely to India for an alliance between them is an often overlooked fact of recent history. It would have been easiest for India to part with Kashmir at that juncture and also easiest for Muslims to obtain such an annulment.

Post 1947 saw an upliftment of Kashmiri Muslims in economic, social, political, and educational levels from the decades of hovering at the bottom. This period of sea-change in their lives is one of the most significant in their six hundred year history. By the 60's they controlled politics, business, and culture. The "employer-employee" relationship between Hindus and Muslims was reversed. Additionally, Muslims benefited from the Indian Government's policy of ingratiation and appeasement with them. They were left undisturbed in the practice of their religion and culture. The protections provided by Article 370 of the Indian Constitution further strongly reinforced their security: economic, political and religious.

The insurgency of Kashmiri Muslims has roots in their psychological rather than political experience. The outward political aggression is a misplaced catharsis of their latent mental conflicts. We have seen Islamic "revolutions" around the world doing the same. Imprisoned by the antiquatedness and narrowness of their religion, as almost all the practitioners of religions are these days, Muslims unable to cope with the alienation and stresses of the modern life have forged an attack on its imperfections, yearning to recoil to the earlier uncorrupted and pristine state of the practice of Islam. Religions operate on a priori basis and can become a barrier to the questioning spirit needed for modern living. Fundamentalism is several stages further removed from the free questioning spirit than the normal level practice of religion. Religious fundamentalism is the most charged and lethal large scale closed faith system in existence at this time. Its foundations lie in the repudiation of modern life tenets: secularism, scientific humanism, and non-religious spirituality. Islamic fundamentalism furthermore rejects women's equality with men.

The identity problem burdened psyche of a Kashmiri Muslim has, additionally, to bear the non-identity problem he has with India. In spite of sharing India's wealth and security, the Kashmiri Muslim has not cultivated an identity with India. This separateness has led to aloofness and mistrust.

A bomb is a mixture of explosive chemicals triggered by an ignition. To the Kashmiri Muslim state of mind seething with turmoil brought upon by the worldwide fundamentalist movement and buffeted by alienation with India was latched the ignition of Pakistan's Kashmir complicity.

Kashmiri Muslims are committing a physical, economic, and mental suicide. The combined destruction will affect their lives for several generations. The children going through the upheaval will nourish aberrant psyches for the rest of their lives and the trauma will hang heavily on the Kashmiri culture for a long time. It is not the religious restrictions, undemocratic politics, or the eccentric economics which form the underpinnings of the turmoil in Kashmir.

Historians, in future, will look upon the present crisis in Kashmir as an upheaval caused by its people due to their long and tortured struggle with their identity, expressed outwardly by a religio-political freedom movement, exploited and abetted fully by its neighbor, Pakistan, which was hungering for long to enclave it to help its internal political problems.

TERRORISM IN KASHMIR SYMPOSIUM

(April 1993)

Promotional letter for the *Terrorism In Kashmir* symposium held on May 8, 1993, in Parsippany, New Jersey.

TERRORISM IN KASHMIR SYMPOSIUM

(SPONSORED BY INDO-AMERICAN KASHMIR FORUM & KASHMIR OVERSEAS ASSOCIATION)

Dear Friend:

A man believes in many things: peace and unconstrained pursuit of happiness, brotherhood of mankind and equality among its groups, and uniqueness of the individual. These are not only lofty visions of mankind but, also, the practical ways to live it has learned in its long history on this planet. When these values are shattered a human being's life is reduced to mere physical existence.

The above devastation in Kashmir is furthermore accompanied by the massacre of an innocent minority and destruction of its property, bringing a total breakdown of civilization. All this is being done in the name of religion.

The Kashmir crisis has reached a point where it is possible that we may lose it in the not so distant future. This calamity will bring unspeakable pain to the two hundred thousand Hindu refugees created by the crisis, dismember India of an ancient and a significant part, and trigger the withering away of a culture.

Even before the materialization of this ultimate catastrophe we are standing in witness to human suffering and degradation of horrific proportions. Two hundred thousand tortured victims are struggling for survival in torment and humiliation. They have mostly met unsympathetic and uncaring treatment by the government. Their misery and hopelessness has left a hole in our hearts and disillusionment in our minds.

What should they do to survive? What will they do tomorrow? Where do they go from here? These are open-ended questions which reverberate in empty echoes, without answers. Human condition at this level provokes anger, heartbreak, compassion, and flight into action.

Toward the end of action many organizations around the world have made contributions. Kashmir Overseas Association, based in U.S.A., has sent more than $100,000 and clothing to the refugees and, also, sent its personnel to their camps to assess the situation firsthand. The Kashmir upheaval is being countered at different levels: political, military, cultural, and intellectual. You most likely have participated at more than one level.

Some people in the Tri-State area think that a symposium on the terrorism in Kashmir will be a valuable contribution to the cause of stemming it. Many non-Kashmir Indians, most Americans, and people of other nationalities are unfamiliar with the causes of the Kashmir crisis. Because of this, most of the people remain on the sidelines, inactive and unmotivated to take any position on the problem. Furthermore, the terrorists and their backers have put forward fractured and imaginatively colored version of the facts. In fact, a well programmed and orchestrated disinformation campaign.

Kashmiris alone cannot fight the war with the religious fundamentalists. We need the help of non-Kashmiri Indians, Americans, and other people. One of the first steps of persuasion is dissemination of information concerning the cause. We believe by presenting information on Kashmir history, causes of the crisis, and the consequences of the terrorism, the American politicians, press, and people, and the people of other nationalities will be better motivated to fight for what is fair and just.

The committee believes that education on the Kashmir crisis is of paramount importance, particularly for the American politicians and the press. Fortified by facts, we can impregnate them with the confidence of conviction.

The Committee plans to present a symposium on terrorism in Kashmir in the next three to four months in New Jersey. American and Indian politicians, others, and you will be invited to speak and participate.

We expect the symposium to inform, persuade, and motivate people to fight for the right of Kashmiri Hindus and other minorities to live peacefully in their homeland and to stop further devastation of Kashmir. Details of the symposium will be sent to you as they develop.

To arrange this symposium we need your organizational and financial help. Please write to the Committee at the given address. Your help of $50, $100, and more is essential for the effort to materialize. Send your checks to Indo-American Kashmir Forum.

It is an extraordinary experience to witness your homeland destroyed, your brethren brutalized, and your culture smitten. But even while going through this harrowing experience one hears the inner voice murmuring: if Kashmir dies can we live, and if we live can we let Kashmir die?

LETTER TO THE
NEW YORK TIMES

(December 12, 1992)

A letter to The New York Times in response to its article on
Kashmir *Where Violence Has Silenced Verse,* published on
November 22, 1992.

LETTER TO THE
NEW YORK TIMES

12.7.92

Letter to The Editor Magazine
The N.Y.Times
229 W, 43 St. New York, N.Y. 10036

Dear Sirs:

An article on a problem facing a few million people, where a lot of them have been killed and continue to be killed, and where uncertainty hangs heavily on their future, deserves an exposition of the causes of the problem. An impressionistic presentation, orchestrated with interviews, and tapesteried with on-the-site photographs, does not go beyond window-dressing for the readers for whom the article has been written, general Americans, who are unfamiliar with not only the complex history of Kashmir problem but, also, with its present tangled situation.

In 1947, Kashmiri Muslims, along with their greatest leader, Sheikh Abdullah, acceded to India: popularly, willfully, and legally though their Constituent Assembly. They rejected unequivocally their choice of joining the other side, Pakistan. Becoming an independent nation was not viable then and is not so now. Their cool-headed decision was based on the long shared history with India, its fervent secularistic principles, the quality of it leadership, and on the religious statehood of

Pakistan. This reasoned decision was richly rewarded by the four decades of their immense prosperity and control over the Valley's commercial, political, and cultural spheres that followed. Indian government was an outsider, incessantly trying to please the local government, to the extent of latter's exploitation of the former. The Muslims on the other side of the border, in Pakistan, lived in perennial economic jaundice coupled with chronic political instability. Sheikh Abdullah was once asked why he chose India over Pakistan for Kashmir to join with. He answered that he opted for the side which offered his people the better economic and political security.

The present turbulence in Kashmir has been masterminded by Pakistan, which has forever lusted for Kashmir, for symbolic and political reasons. The latter has been to divert the attention of its people from the inexorable political abyss it has always been in. It is also due to the echo of the world-wide Islamic fundamentalist movement, which got its greatest impetus from the Iranian revolution.

The upheaval gripping Kashmir does not represent a revolution like the one we had in Iran or the Kurdish movement in force in Iraq. It is a grand scale mischief perpetrated by Pakistan and, above all, it is a manifestation of ineptitude of the Indian government and the weakness of its leaders.

Upheaval In Kashmir

(May 1990)

An analysis of the 1989 eruption of civil war in Kashmir.

UPHEAVAL IN KASHMIR

"Science without religion is lame, religion without science is blind."–A. Einstein.

The eruption of turmoil in Kashmir has uncovered one more religious fundamentalist wound in the world. Some of the 3 million Muslims there, who make up 85% of the population, would like to form an Islamic republic, or join one, Pakistan, which is conveniently a contiguous neighbor.

Religion has been one of the preeminent components of man's mental infrastructure from even before the emergence of civilization. At its highest level it has provided the psychological and moral basis for human life, the vision, the values, and the motivation for living. But because it operates on a priori and unquestioning basis its driving force is visionary emotion and not the architecture of reasoning. As Stefan Zweig said, "Every conscience wishes the death of every other conscience," the absolute character of religion has created much killing and suffering in mankind. Many a page in human history is soaked in the blood of religious massacres. Man has learned a lot by his experience and yet his propensity to forget the lessons he has learned is enormous. That is why all civilized countries separate the governance of people from the practice of religion.

To the ills of poverty, disease, ignorance, and slavery facing mankind add another: religious fundamentalism. Its driving force is insecurity and narcissism. Fundamentalists want to live by the purity of the vision of God, a simplistic and a fairy tale mental existence, where the major ordering factors of life come only in binary logic: good, evil; right, wrong; heaven, hell; life, death. Everything comes in either black or white, the gray shades do not exist. Muslim fundamentalists want to go back to the old ways of Islamic life and Koranic laws, while the rest of the world is trying to find a new way to live and a new social understanding. They see evil in science and technology, freedom of women, and irreligious enjoyment of life. Finding a lot of the world holding different visions of life they want to recoil back within their own group, insulated from change. They find scientific thinking threatening the security of their world. Their half-hearted attempts to go along with the modern life have produced enough confusion in them to want to go back wholeheartedly to the ancient way of living. Religious fundamentalism is the last ditch effort to stem the spreading wave of the western style scientific humanism. To live life on the principles of equality of all men and to pursue personal happiness in a natural way, and to approach the understanding of life, the world, and the universe in a scientific fashion has been the greatest setback to religious way of living. Fundamentalists believe that the highest state of their religion can be achieved by the literal observance of its codes and that the pristine glow of their spiritual vision can be realized by the unwavering and the relentless pursuit of their faith.

Extremist religious organizations invariably interpret their religious books literally rather than coming to grips with the metaphor behind the text. Philosophy is not emphasized enough to raise the level of understanding among the common followers. Along with the zealots there are opportunists who exploit the economically downtrodden to pursue their goals of power and economic profit.

In the reckless pursuit of their fantasies, the militants in Kashmir have ignored the civil rights of minorities, notably a half-million Buddhists living in the higher valleys of Ladakh, one hundred and fifty thousand Hindus and Sikhs living in Srinagar and its environs, and one and a half million Hindus living in the southern part of the state called Jammu. The Muslims constitute 60% of the population of the state of Jammu and Kashmir.

Selected Hindu civil servants perceived to be the enemies of the fundamentalists cause have been gunned down. A state of terror reigns over the valley of Kashmir and all the offices, businesses, and schools have remained closed for last four months, without a hope of reopening in immediate future. There is round the clock military curfew, paralyzing the life. There are no negotiations going on with the government as the fundamentalists have no intentions to do so. They have no publicly known leaders. With summer tourism revenues of $350 million dollars lost this year the future is catastrophic. This nightmarish situation has been going on for a third of a year now and the end is nowhere in sight. Hindus and other minorities are locking up their residences and fleeing the valley of death. Chaos, paralysis, and fear have reduced the life for most of the people to an indefinite house-arrest.

Bars, movie halls and video parlors in Srinagar, the summer capital of the state, have been closed at gun-point, as they are considered the means of moral ruination. Women are being forced to cover their faces to let men keep their lust in check, bearing resemblance to post-Afghan invasion era in the state.

Kashmiris are an independent-minded people, timid but egotistical, sensitive but proud, non-conformist but practical. The roots of Kashmiri culture are deeply interconnected with India as far back as 3000 B.C. The Muslims took root in Kashmir in Shah Mir's time in 1339 A.D. and this was followed by a turmoil filled era under the Chaks, the Mougals, and the Afghans, when a systematic genocide of the masses in Srinagar and its environs was undertaken by a number of ruthless rulers. A brief breather was provided when Pandit Birbal Dhar sought the help of the Sikh Maharaja Ranjeet Singh, whose armies routed the Pathans at Shopian in 1819 A.D. The Sikh governors generally proved to be tough masters. This was followed by the Dogra rule when Maharaja Gulab Singh acquired Kashmir through the sale from the British in 1846 and the state of Jammu and Kashmir was born. Before the Indian independence in 1947, the Rajas, the

Maharajas, and the Nawabs of approximately 600 autonomous states were given the choice of joining either secular India or Muslim Pakistan or to remain independent. Surprisingly, Maharaja Han Singh of Jammu and Kashmir did not join the union of India until the Kabailis (tribesmen) backed by Pakistan army invaded the state. The King fled Srinagar on October 25, 1947 and signed the letter of accession to India on October 26, 1947. The Indian troops were sent to Srinagar with the consent of the popular Muslim leader, Sheikh M. Abdullah, on October 27. They repulsed the attackers up to only sixty miles from Srinagar at Uri. India had acquired a beautiful though a perilous gift. It could not let go the prize, but did not know the price it would have to pay to keep it.

The Indian strategy was to keep this underdeveloped state economically protected and its borders with Pakistan secure. The Indian government paid heavy bills for it and passed a special amendment in its national constitution (Article 370) to protect the state further by disallowing outsiders to buy property in it. A large majority of Kashmiri Muslims and some Hindus prospered immensely in the four decades that followed. The strategy worked most of the time but extracted a heavy toll from India. By pampering Kashmiris all the time they became bereft of the sense of responsibility a citizen owes its state. Greed stifled their development as equal partners of their state. Though enjoying the attention they were getting, some of them never renounced their desire to form an Islamic state or join one. In fact, there was always a veiled threat to revert to their desire if Indian Government did not continue the son-in-law treatment of them. This sordid relationship of purchased loyalty is the essence of the problem. Forty years of support, care, and pampering by India has not dulled the Islamic propensity of some Kashmiri Muslims to live in a pure state of their ethos, unmixed with other religious communities. Muslim communities around the world would like to do the same. After passing away of the popular Muslim leader, Sheikh Abdullah, and with the proliferation of Islamic upheavals in the world, the separatist movement found a good climate to grow in. The last chief Minister Farooq Abdullah's chaotic and permissive leadership provided a strong catalyst to it. The victories of the Sikhs fighting their cause in the neighboring Punjab provided further encouragement. What was merely an excitement triggering sport for a few unemployed youth only four years ago, due to local governments negligence, in fact permissiveness, mushroomed into a fundamentalist force.

The recent meeting of the terrorist's demands by the government in exchange for the freedom of federal Home Minister's kidnapped daughter was the spark which ignited the movement's powder-keg. While the watershed political movements in Europe are leading the way from totalitarian systems toward democracy and secularism, the present rebellion in Kashmir is aspiring to achieve the identity of a people through a religious state.

What should a nation do in such a situation? There are hundreds of separatist movements round the world, some have gone public, others are still under cover. Each has a unique history and present circumstances. We cannot meet every separatist group's call, under the reasoning that freedom is better than forced coexistence. Each case has to be evaluated on its merits. We cannot let nations be dismembered because of identification problems of one group with the rest of the groups in the community. In the long run, such separatist movements may do more harm than good to its people. Discipline required to coexist, difficult and even painful at times, may be rewarding.

In Kashmir, the present revolution is not even aimed at democracy, which exists there at the same superficial level as it does in the rest of India, it is pointed toward gaining ascendancy to a total religious way of living, in state, public, and personal spheres.

Articles On Kashmir

These six articles were written on a visit to Kashmir in August 2011, after a gap of nine years.

FLEETING MOMENTS AT PAHALGAM

It was August 15, I was going to Pahalgam after 23 years. Besides the overriding urge to see a beloved place, I was also keen to see the changes in it, that time inexorably brings to almost everything.

Some very happy moments of my life have occurred in Pahalgam. Human happiness is a very complex thing: it can depend upon the circumstances of one's social, economical, and physical lives; the point at which one is at in one's self-discovery and one's goals in life. Needless to say, being in Pahalgam itself must have been a very big catalyst in those moments.

My van passed Anantnag by the bypass road and almost everything about the road had changed: width, quality, traffic, and shops. The change was so sweeping that I even missed spotting my in-laws' former house. Getting closer to Mattan, I was excited by the anticipation of it, but it never appeared, because we were on a new Mattan bypass road. On the way to Pahalgam we pass by many villages and hamlets. They seem so human and primitive that I felt that I should stop at each one of them, to walk through their lanes, do window-shopping, and perhaps talk with some people. The idea of their simplicity: lack of sophistication, guilelessness, and directness were very attractive human attributes for me, especially coming that I was from a highly materialistic, self-centered, and self-conscious culture. But I was unable to stop and indulge in my fancy due to the paucity of time.

For most of the trip, from just a few miles outside Srinagar to many miles before Pahalgam, there is a backdrop of the high mountains. This special drapery gave not only the particular road I was travelling on, but to the whole valley of Kashmir, a special aura. Just journeying anywhere within the valley is a special treat.

Getting close of the periphery of Pahalgam spurted my excitement high. Suddenly, a corner of the familiar ring of the mountains around Pahalgam appeared, followed gradually by the entire ring. *Here I was again in Pahalgam!* The incredibility of this fact kept me nagging for several minutes, till my subconscious finally admitted that I was in Pahalgam. We quickly passed through the downtown, a strip of contiguous shops, on an arched road. Within a few moments of passing through the bazaar I concluded that almost all of them had undergone changes; either they were rebuilt or were upgraded. Shop signs announcing Kashmiri shawls and handicrafts swarmed swiftly. Horses, highly emaciated, with or without riders on them, dotted the scene. That there were not a large number of tourists in Pahalgam was no surprise to me, as *Amarnath Yatra* had just ended, on Aug. 12. The lineup of the big three hotels: Hotel Pahalgam, Woodstock, Mountview, on the left side of the main street became visible. After the fleeting initial view of Pahalgam, I directed my mind to find out quickly where I was going to stay. From my homework about it in Srinagar I had concluded that besides the three hotels just mentioned, one could also stay in Grand Mumtaz. My taxi driver suggested considering staying in a hut too. We quickly went to see them and after looking up one of them I decided they were not good enough. After that we went to Mountview and I was shown an available room, which the hotel management said had the better view of Pahalgam compared to others. I liked it at once. Because of the view it commands, its location, and the quality of its rooms, Mountview is one of the better places to stay in Pahalgam.

Years back Mountview Hotel was called Wazir Hotel; then in 1987 its young manager suffered a heart attack, compelling him to sell it. But the name Wazir Hotel had already been changed to

Mountview Hotel. In 1995 the hotel suffered a big fire, resulting in its rebuilding.

Immediately after checking in the hotel I went to view the central area of Pahalgam, which I call its "face." I saw the gushing Liddar swarming over the continuous bed of rocks strewn over its path. It is an enchanting sight, one of the salient features of Pahalgam's beauty. Lifting my eyes from the river I saw the magnificent presence of the ring of the mountains surrounding Liddar. In fact, Liddar without these mountains would not have amounted to much. I realized that Pahalgam, essentially, was still the same as it was 23 years ago, because the mountains and Liddar had not changed, which comprised its essence; rest of the elements were insignificant. The beauty of the mountains is greatly enhanced by the tapestry of the gracefully tall and slender pine trees.

Looking at the "face" of Pahalgam I felt that it was just an unsophisticated patch of land, bald at many places, with weeds growing at other places, just a few flower beds adorning it. What a waste of a great opportunity! Here was a place which could have been turned into a beautiful garden, having benches in it, sitting on which one could linger on the magnificent valley around. The state government, the custodian of the land, has not thought much about beautifying it. They have thought that keeping the land free of commercial and private buildings is the highest care they can bestow upon it. Their lack of imagination has been a great disservice to Pahalgam, the top attractor of visitors going to Kashmir. It could have called for proposals to landscape the area from internationally renowned park landscapers, and then the winning design could have been implemented locally. The state has followed such a route in the development of tunnels and a cable-car project. Exactly the same is the fate of the Gulmarg "face."

I took a trip to Aru, a hamlet about 8 miles from Pahalgam. Throughout the journey the scene was so lonely that you felt nature whispering in your ears, "I am here." Magnificent views of Liddar valley are present. I repeated taking a photograph of the site that I had taken 37 years ago, but the results showed that the earlier one was superior. Aru is a very low-key hamlet, which only swells to life during Amarnath *Yatra.* I could not but think of the life the local people, *Gujars,* lead. They are a nomadic people, who live in the mountains. It is quite apparent that they lead a very simple life, shorn of the fuss we city dwellers make. Above all, they lead a truer life. Living on bare essentials, in the intimate company of nature, they feel the pulse of life which many "civilized" people do not.

There are many new hotels in Pahalgam ; among them Grand Mumtaz is one of the better ones. A beautiful golf course has been constructed last year, which happens to be next to the hotel. The downtown has expanded at the town entrance area. Some roads have changed. Pahalgam is not a place for entertainment, that is, there are no bars, nightclubs, casinos, movie halls, etc. Because of the prohibition on serving alcohol, no hotel can serve it, and there are no shops selling it either. So, the drink lovers feels unfairly punished, but the smart ones among them bring their liquor with them. In my short experience in Pahalgam I did not have much luck with the quality of food. Dinner at Woodstock was a disaster, experience at Mountview was just a little better. A Hotel Pahalgam restaurant (outside it) did not serve Kashmiri cuisine.

Pahalgam is a dreamy place, as is the characteristic of most of the Kashmir scenery. No wonder that has influenced Kashmiris to be dreamers. We can also say that Kashmiri scenery is meditative, but that has not helped Kashmiris to be so in the modern times, though in the ancient times they were steeped in it.

Memories of the past numerous trips to Pahalgam flashed in my mind. In 1959 I spent about six weeks here with my uncle, who was the chief physician of this place at that time. I was in a transition between my appearance in the intermediate college exams and their results. My parents and siblings were in Cairo, Egypt. Here was an interlude free of work, social responsibilities, and stress of any kind. It was as if I was travelling in a boat, on a calm river, surrounded by breathtaking scenery, journeying without a destination. My uncle and I were the only two occupants in his apartment for some time, which later changed with the arrival of his niece, with whom I got along very well. Day after day was an enchanting experience. I fell under the spell of a nurse working under my uncle. The sadness of her life penetrated me deeply and stayed with me for many years. Even more than the circumstances of her life, I was struck with the way she was facing them. She lived her life with a calm dignity and heroic acceptance of the tragedy. She had a poet's appreciation of life. For years I wanted to meet her again but the practical difficulties hindered that.

I was also reminded of my trip here in 1974 when my parents and another uncle and aunt were with me. It was a splendid vacation for more than one reason: right time in life, right company, right mood. All the four have left the world. Each one of them was a special person. Only the memory of their personalities, conversations, time spent together, and good deeds remain.

Every day I went out for morning walks to Liddar bank, looking at the marvel of the total scene, feeling that man was not alone, he was in company of a lofty spirit.

On Aug. 17, two days after arriving in Pahalgam, I decided that I must move on to the next place in my ambitious trip to Kashmir. Much as it made me sad that I was walking away too soon from one of my most beloved places, but I had no choice.

The fleeting moments in Pahalgam had revived my old self, dreams, and love of life, even as they were accompanied with some of my old pains.

On leaving Pahalgam I felt pretty confident that I will be returning to it in not too distant future.

SIESTA AT MANSBAL LAKE

On a weekday, in the early afternoon, I reached Mansbal Lake. It is a small, pearl of a lake, placid, unpretentious. Its appearance and size makes you connect with it quickly. Unlike its famous sister, Dal Lake, Manasbal Lake is easier to understand and absorb. There were only a couple of dozen people in it during my visit. The mood was that of opulent tranquility, tender dreaminess.

Considered the deepest lake in Kashmir, at a maximum depth of 43 ft., it has engendered a myth that it is bottomless. A prodigious field of lotuses adorns it, which also makes it one of the largest sources of *nadrus* (lotus stalk), a popular item of Kashmiri cuisine. Then this is also among the top places to view aquatic birds. So many attributes for one splendid body of water.

After taking a wide and deep look at the lake and also taking all the photographs that I wanted to take, I decided to skip seeing the two important auxiliaries of the lake: a Mughal Garden, called *Jarokha,* built by Moghul queen Noor Jahan and the ruins of a 17th century fort called Darogabagh, also built by Moghuls, which used to serve as an inn for travelers journeying between Punjab and Srinagar.

Moved by the supine serenity of the place and privacy afforded by the virtual absence of people, I decided that I must take a nap under a tree, an image of bliss conjured up from my childhood.

I was very surprised by the choice of my activity, but I was being propelled by an inner force. I managed to land my aging frame on the ground, wrapped my camera round my right arm, and closed my eyes. I was amazed to see the *Lady Sleep* slowly curling her arms around me; I passed quickly thereafter. When I opened my eyes I saw that I had been in the other world for 45 minutes. Clearly Manasbal Lake inspired me to ignore everything: time of the day, public location, busy schedule, my past inability to sleep during daytime, and took me in her arms. That was incredible to me, as I am almost never able to sleep during daytime. I was quite elated by my performance because coming from a materialistic culture, in which people are always looking at their watches, to find enough inspiration and peace of mind to cut myself off from the world was no easy task.

I took a few more photographs and once again looked deep into the lake, to absorb its spirit and charisma. Slowly, but reluctantly, I walked toward my waiting taxi. On the way to Dal Gate we passed through many villages and hamlets, and the town of Ganderbal. People looked so much simpler and less stressed than their counterparts in the Western societies.

The siesta at Manasbal Lake started to sink in me, and I realized it was one of the defining moments of my trip to Kashmir, for it symbolized that I had arrived at a stage in my life, when I could distance myself from the material universe around me for some time.

In Search Of The Soul Of Gulmarg

It had been 25 years since I had visited Gulmarg. My urge to revisit it was intense, but more intense than that was to find its soul; because I had always wondered why many people thought it to be the epitome of the Kashmir vacation places; even greater than Pahalgam.

On August 17 I reluctantly departed from Pahalgam and headed almost straight to Gulmarg, except for a brief stopover in Srinagar.

Leaving Srinagar we took Highway IA, a major highway in J & K. Beyond Srinagar airport, into Bemina, a fast developing suburb, we drove toward Gulmarg. The highway up to about Bemina was a 4-lane road, which I was told was going to be expanded into a 6-lane road. Kashmir was finally coming of age to become a user-oriented place.

On the way to Gulmarg, my taxi driver stopped at an orchid. The buxom apples, ripening into red skin, which was enveloping a still-developing rich juiciness. One was tempted to pluck them.

Tangmarg, the stop before Gulmarg, existing in the shadow of Gulmarg's glory, has a personality of its own. There are visitors who like to stay in it, for its charms, facilities, and its self-effacing image. It is the headquarters of the military guarding Gulmarg, which is close to Pakistan. No military stays in Gulmarg, to give the tourists a chance to forget the Kashmir Problem for a little while. The road between Tangmarg and Gulmarg has seen a great upgrade since I travelled on it last. You find pines and other trees on it, setting up an aura of natural glory of the entire area.

At the end of the Tangmarg-Gulmarg road one suddenly sees a vast panoramic site of a natural meadow, circumferenced by tall, graceful mountains, dotted by magnificently tall and slender pine trees. This is the Gulmarg of the legends and tourism literature.

The central area of Gulmarg is a natural bowl, green but with many bald spots and weeds on it. It is 1.86 square miles area, with a length of 1.8 and a width of 0.62 miles. The average altitude of Gulamrg is 8, 825 ft., its highest point is 13,780 ft., at Apharwat mountain. Looking at just the "face "of Gulmarg, one is puzzled by its reputation as the best tourist place in Kashmir.

During spring Gulmarg meadow is swamped with bluebells, daisies, forget-me-nots, and buttercups, to the extent that it made the last Sultan of Kashmir, Yusuf Shah Chak (ruled 1579-86), to change its name from Gaurimarg (Gauri was Lord Shiva's consort) to Gulmarg, which in Urdu means a meadow of flowers. (*marg* means meadow) The king may have been ignorant of the significance of its original name and insensitive to smothering its history; like many kings of earlier times, his personal emotion was generally more important than anything else. The romantic Mughal king Jahangir(1569-1627) was also a lover of Gulmarg. Aurel Stein, the noted British archeologist (who among other things discovered the text of *Diamond Sutra),* lived in a tent in Gulmarg, between his field trips.

In the modern times, British rediscovered Gulmarg, in 1927; establishing the golf club, which still exists. It became a hot vacation spot for the colonizers, including its military. They found the snow-bound slopes of Gulmarg a fit place to expend their passions for nature and sports.

The central valley of Gulmarg, the meadow that has given it its name, has been poorly landscaped; in fact it has not been landscaped at all, just left "natural." Many beautiful things could have been done to it: conversion to a park, embedded with organized flower-beds, trees, plants, walking-paths, benches, etc. The finished product would be a sophisticated garden blending with the basic scenery of Gulmarg, which is high mountains, embroidered with high pine trees. Instead of that what we have is a nearly two square miles of a primitive landscape. The custodian of Gulmarg, the state government, thinks that by leaving it "natural" it is imparting Gulmarg the greatest artistry. Internationally reputed public park landscapers have to be invited to submit proposals for the drastic facelift of the Gulmarg's "face."

Gulmarg has about 40 hotels, some good, others sunk into mediocrity. But it has no downtown: no good shops, no bars. The only whiff of a downtown that it has is a rambling, primitive bazaar. The absence of bars is due to the prohibition on alcohol, to an extent that only one state-run liquor store is allowed, which was closed due to the ongoing Ramadan. Without some sort of entertainment, besides golfing and skiing, the vacationers, after soaking nature for most of the time, feel bored.

My search for the soul of Gulmarg made me realize that it does not so much lie in its central meadow, but in its higher level places of Khilanmarg valley, Apharwat mountain, Alpather lake, and beyond. This area is like the forehead of Gulmarg, while its central meadow its bosom. From here you see the majestic sweep of the pine forests and beyond them the valley of Kashmir. On a clear day one can see the mountains Nanga Parbat (26,660 ft., in Pakistan) and Harmukh (16,870 + ft.) The grandeur of the views afforded transport you to a higher level experience of nature, creating a mood of enchantment, wonder, awe, and selflessness.

It is the Upper Gulmarg (a name I am giving to the ensemble of places at the higher altitudes than the main meadow of Gulmarg) that attracts Gulmarg's most ardent admirers, the skiers. Gulmarg is one of the top skiing places in the world, because of its high altitude, the length of its skiing track, and the scenery it commands. From December to March, Gulmarg is converted to a vast skiing arena, bringing glory to the place, as well as money to the entrepreneurs. The irony is that through the skiing fame of Gulmarg, the government tries to lure tourists to the other parts of Kashmir, which may be more beautiful than Gulmarg.

All the high success of Upper Gulmarg would not have been possible without the cable car system, called Gondola here, which was installed in 1998. It ferries skiers, trekkers, and general purpose tourists from the Gulmarg base station, at 8,530 ft. elevation, to Kongdoori (in Khilanmarg valley), in its first stage. In the second stage, which opened in 2005, Gondola goes from Kongdoori to a station at 12,959 ft., near Apharwat mountain peaks. The highest point of Gulmarg is at 13,780 ft., at a peak of Apharwat mountain. Gondala was engineered by the French company Pomagalski. Because of the success of skiing, another cable car system running parallel to the second stage of Gondola, which will run from Kongdoori to a place called Mary's Shoulder, in Apharwat mountain peaks, is being planned by the company. It will cater to beginner and intermediate-level skiers. Gondola fares are low. Horse owners and guides are fighting with the government for compensation to them for the loss to their trades due to the Gondola.

I stayed in hotel Grand Mumtaz, a reasonably good place. I walked to the downtown bazaar, rather than take a taxi or horse, to feel the grounds of Gulmarg and contemplate its scene better. There is a 7 mile road which goes round Gulmarg, called Outer Ring Road, providing a walk through pine forests and affording panoramic views of Kashmir valley and mountains that are also visible from Upper Gulmarg. Gulmarg has a golf course, at 8,694 ft., touted to be either at the highest altitude or among the top group of high altitude golf courses in the world. It is very interesting, and lends to good reason, that for security reasons, due to its proximity to Pakistan, that no local people can stay for nights in Gulmarg, except for hotel operators and critical government personnel. The population is only 664.

In Gulmarg one's sight gazes at distant panoramic horizons, while at Pahalgam it is more restricted. This gives Gulmarg a greater visual heft, which translates into a more spiritual and romantic experience. In the arms of nature one feels the hand of something higher, a tug for something impersonal.

Following day I packed my stuff and drove down through the meadow of Gulmarg, onto to the steep Gulmarg-Tangmarg road. Going downhill on this road indicates a departure from Gulmarg, the queen of panoramic sights, where the romance with the mountains leaves an everlasting impression on one's life. I bade goodbye to Gulmarg reluctantly, for I had just discovered what its soul is and where it lay, and I needed some more time to absorb that.

TOUCHING THE REMNANTS OF TIME
IN OLD SRINAGAR

On August 19, at about noon, I was in front of the house I was born at several decades ago. While experiencing the moment I could feel the flow of time. This was the place where the clock of my life started ticking. I was born at my maternal grandfather's house, which was inhabited by six Karihalloo brothers and their families. The joint household was so large that in the evening an attendance would be taken of the youngsters to make sure none them were missing after an afternoon of games and fun. I became the beloved grandchild of my grandfather, Dama Kaul Karihalloo, by virtue of the transference of his love for his favorite daughter, Arni, who was renowned for her fine demeanor, charming shyness, and beauty.

The Karihalloo house was located at Fateh Kadal, near Malik Angan. Relying on my photographic memory of places, I looked for the right lane to turn into, but was prevented to find it, by the changes that several decades since my last visit to my birthplace had wrought to its neighborhood. Finally, I resorted to asking people on the street for the direction to the Karihalloo house. When it seemed that no one could help me, an old man, perhaps in his 80's, confidently told me that he could help me. I requested him if he could walk me up to the house, instead of giving me its directions. He enthusiastically escorted me to my destination; without him I would have had difficulties in finding it. All the markers I had remembered for the house had been swallowed by the vortex of time. One of the salient markers of the house,

the Madan house, which was in close proximity, I was unable
to locate. The people living in the house after Karihalloo's had
taken a good care of it, as it looked intact, as well as spruced
up. I conjured up the images of the halcyon days of Karihalloos,
living in familial bliss and with a strong identity, unlike most of
the families in the Age Of Technology we live in. I mused on why
and when I was orphaned from the clan, detached from the hub.

I went to see the house in Malikyar where I spent most of my
childhood and young adulthood, just up to the point of leaving
college for a professional college outside Kashmir. I thought I
knew the road from Karan Nagar to my house, having traversed it
several thousand times. While the starting point was identifiable
but as my taxi went along the road it changed drastically. We
continued on it, not knowing any better, till we hit the new Fateh
Kadal, called Biscoe Bridge; having a good idea of the location of
the bridge from my previous visit, I thought I would know how to
reach my house. So, the taxi driver followed my directions, until
we discovered we were lost. This was a shock to my confidence.
While making inquiries from the people on the street, an old man
gave me the directions, but he wondered who I was. Upon giving
him my identity, he got very excited, and later emotional, as he
revealed his. He was our neighbor Omar Bhat, he and his family
had lived across our street for decades. We hugged each other and
later we met again outside our former house.

Seeing my former house I was excited but also a little
disappointed, as its appearance had changed. It had a new color
on the outside, as well as a new roof, the windows also appeared
to have changed. I started taking pictures of the house and its
environs. Khet Beni's green grocery shop was no longer there, as
were not the butcher, *kandar wan,* Khala *bisot's,* and Shudhar's
dry grocery shops. To say that the neighborhood had changed was
an understatement; it had drastically changed. But the roads were
better built, including the old feces-laden lanes. I was happy to
see the lane near my house, which I used to take to go to college
and other places, made *pukka.* In the old days, walking over it,
especially in dark, was a risk I had no choice but to take. Our

immediate neighbor, Khatbeni's (different from the green grocer) family, had moved to suburbs (Khatbeni herself had died in 70's). But for the mosque and woodwork shop, every other shop had changed, although the street and lane layout had remained the same. There was an open area we called *bagh* where we used to play, the only decent playground we had; it was now occupied by a new house. This seemed to be an encroachment from the point of view of my sentiments for the *bagh.* I was feeling *how could they?* Within a few minutes after my arrival on the scene several people gathered around me, who later I came to know were my old neighbors. Now old like me, they had changed, as I must have appeared to them. I did not recognize anyone of them, as they must not have recognized me. After introductions we were excited and the emotions gushed. Some of them wanted me to have tea with them right away. I had to tell them that I would come another day and would be happy to spend time with them, but time is a merciless maiden who must keep you on a leash to suit her agenda.

Ghulam Mohamad Durzi, the person to whom my uncle sold our former house, was in the small group of people who surrounded me once the word went out in the *mohalla* that I was there. He seemed to be a fine gentleman: courteous and low-key. I asked him if I could visit my former house; he graciously invited me to visit it. We entered the house where I had spent 14 years of my early life. The years in which I came to know something of human desire, relationships, and loneliness. The years that laid the foundation of my consciousness and launched the odyssey of my search for the absolute. Here was the house where I had secretly cried, was smitten with loneliness, as I was left by my parents at my uncle's house, under the idea that remaining in Srinagar, rather than in New Delhi, where they were stationed at that time, would help my education. The seeds of my loneliness were sown earlier than they should have been. All these early experiences have contributed to what I have grown up to be now, warts-and-all.

Escorted courteously by Darzi Sahib, we went room by room in my former home. Our *wut* was shortened by including some of its space with the newly designed kitchen. Gone was the old earthen *dhaan,* replaced by a table-top type of range. The *betakh* had remained unchanged and the *muttey koothar,* the grain storage room, was where it used to be. On the second floor I passed by the *koothar* where I used to study. I went in the *bud kuth,* where my parents Babuji and Bhabi used to sleep. I looked out from one of its windows at the bazaar outside. The wooden *jali* below the window, where once my right hand got stuck in one of its spaces, needing an emergency intervention of someone to free it, was no longer there. Similarly, on the third floor I looked out from my uncle Papaji's bedroom. The house looked now so much smaller than it seemed to be when I lived there. Time, for a moment, seemed to have frozen, and I traversed forward and backward on its wings.

From the *kaani* I looked over to my uncles' houses and was shocked to see them splintered badly, as if a hurricane had smothered them. I asked my host what had happened. He explained that the destruction was the work of militants sometime back. I did not feel comfortable asking him the details, as they would have necessarily upset him. But what was surprising to me was that by 2002 these houses were purchased by Muslim families, but were yet destroyed by militants. Furthermore, the compound between our house and the uncles' houses was rife with weeds, as the lack of its use over extended time would have encouraged. The site of these houses was painful, flashing in my mind momentarily the turbulent history of the last two decades.

While going through my house a memory of an event spontaneously crossed my mind. During one afternoon in 50's I had just heard the announcement of my expected passing of the matriculation examination. Jubilantly I marched to Amira Kadal to indulge in some celebration with my friends. On the way I fell from a bicycle and broke my left arm. Seething with pain, I cancelled the celebration and walked to my *matamal* at Mandir Bagh to sleep off my pain. But its accentuation compelled me to visit a neighborhood hospital, Rattan Rani Hospital. Screening revealed a fracture of the elbow. Burdened with the grim news I marched to my home. Upon hearing my travail, some people present at my home that time talked about setting the elbow bones by the traditional bone setting procedure, which involved first breaking the joint in question in a rice pounding stone vat and then setting it right, of course without the use of anesthesia. I was smitten with fear at the scenario but luckily when my uncle Papaji came home he dismissed this barbaric procedure and told me he was going to take me to a hospital the following day for the scientifically established state of the art remedy.

We drove over Biscoe Bridge. Then I walked on the old Fateh Kadal, whose width has been reduced to just about 15 ft., for pedestrian use only. From there we drove toward Habba Kadal, formerly the "Times Square" of Srinagar. Passing through Chinkral Mohalla, I keenly looked for the Tarakh Halwoy shop, which sadly did not exist anymore. Again, we have the "pedestrian only" old Habba Kadal, though of full former width. There is a barrier put on the side opposite the Kanya Kadal side, for security reasons. Gone are Kapoor Booksellers and Dr. Chagtoo's office. I walked on the old Habba Kadal and recaptured the times when I along with many boys would watch the girls returning to their homes after a day at school. For me the special moment would come when Bimla and I would stare at each other to carry on our eyes-only romance. The magic of the life on the old Habba Kadal has vanished into the layers of time.

The road between Fateh Kadal and Kralkhud, which used to be too narrow for its usage, has been widened and is of superior quality than before. At Kralkhud I looked up my relatives Shangloo's former home. I saw a woman sitting at the second floor window, which somehow disturbed my concentration to take pictures. Kashmiris have a serious problem of staring at the outsiders. They are unaware that this action is rude behavior. 99% of the times I am able to ignore it and remain focused on taking pictures. This time I momentarily lost my will, with the result I did not take all the pictures I wanted to take. Furthermore,

I did not go inside the Shangloo compound, which I had keenly planned to do.

Moving on further I went to Ganpatyar, where my *poofi* Bengashi used to live. My former markers for the house were nowhere in sight, as the area had changed in the decades I was away. Then I got an idea that I could get the whereabouts of the Muthu household from the people inside the Ganpatyar temple. I was surprised to see the temple had a military camouflage over it and a security check post, obviously to keep the militants away, as it is one of their prime targets for bombardment. Inside the temple, I found a marble floor tile close to the steps leading to the temple idol chamber, inscribed with my *poofa Dr.* Dwarika Nath Muthu's name. This triggered a flashback of my noble uncle, who lived with high integrity and compassion for the destitute.

Beyond Ganpatyar we drove to Mandir Bagh, a place near Rattan Rani Hospital, where Karihalloos lived after they moved from Fateh Kadal. The place had changed drastically. The Karihalloo house had been replaced, a lane built through its garden, and the neighboring Saraf house replaced by a hotel. I remembered the happy childhood days spent at my *matamaal*. My foremost memory is that of my grandfather Baijee, whose acute love for me remains a treasure of my life. Then there was the thrill of spending time with an extended family and playing in the *bamzoonth bagh.*

Following day I went to Amar Singh College, where I had spent three years. Its entrance gate had been moved to the far front side of its main building. Certainly an improvement. At the time of my visit there, about 9 A.M., there were not many students in it, perhaps because it was yet too early for the classes to begin. Again a change from my days.

The building looked as stately and intact as ever to my surprise, as I had expected the inexorable saw of time to have withered it. What could have avoided that in this case of a circa 1930's building? Excellent original design and maintenance. It buoyed my spirits to find that some things used to be done right in the past and then maintained right. The new entrance path bordered with slim and tall poplar trees looked graceful. Overall, the "campus" looked neat. Looking at the field where I had spent countless hours playing cricket, I saw a few cows lazily chewing grass; a not so unusual a sight in India. Some construction was going in the field. Turning to the inside of the building, the "U" contoured back side, where we spent hours waiting for the classes to start, watching girls, or just gossiping, had remained unchanged. I entered one of the unoccupied classrooms and was amazed to see that it had remained in form and shape the same as it was in 1958. It was amusing to see the department and building signs reading: Computer Lab, Health Fitness Centre, etc., the icons of modern culture.

Karan Nagar, formerly a bastion of middle class residence, has absorbed some business activity. Its central boulevard has changed to become one of the heavily trafficked roads in Srinagar. Lal Chowk is Jammu and Kashmir State's most famous square, both politically and commercially. Also, I think, it is the widest road in the state. But the iconic traffic island does not exist anymore. Mir Pan Shop is larger than before and continues to enjoy a special status among the businesses around it. Bund has ceased to be the exciting and fashionable boulevard that it once was, it is sparsely visited now. There are no cinema halls in Srinagar anymore; people see movies through DVDs and TV. J & K prohibition laws only allow two hotels, Lalit Grand Palace and Broadway, to serve alcohol, and 5 state run shops to sell liquor. The latter are closed during the month of Ramadan, when I was there.

Jehlum looks sullen, as there seems to be little activity either on it or at its shores. Its muddy looking waters do not invoke a good mood either. The houses on its shores have a deserted look, with some of them splintered, strongly suggesting their ownership belonging to the Pandits who left them to go out of the state to save their lives. The idea of taking a boat ride down Jehlum that had occurred to me once remained a nonstarter after I viewed its appearance and mood.

The Old Srinagar has changed quite a bit in the last several decades. Apart from the replacement of the major bridges: Fateh Kadal, Habba Kadal, and Zero Bridge, while the old bridges still remain for restricted use, many old roads have also been replaced, and some new roads have been added. New roads are of better quality. Amira Kadal is for pedestrian traffic only.

Tongas are a relic of the old times, the auto rickshaw has taken over. In spite of the strong diktat of the militants to use *burqas*, Kashmiri women defied it, except some of them still use them out of their volition. Their courage is stupendous, their vision is correct. People in general use sneakers, jeans, and T-shirts. The move to suburbs is ongoing. Bemina, beyond the airport, is one of the growing suburbs. Good life concept is sinking in the people.

Shops are bursting with goods, people are bristling with energy, the arrow of time is darting forward. Kashmir is a state in flux. People want to forget the wounds of the recent past, they want to be only dealing with present and future.

The Old Srinagar, like old New York, or old London, or old Delhi is roped in by time, circumscribed by history. It is a living museum, where the patina of time has given everything coloration, where we cannot expect any significant changes to occur. It is only the archeologists, historians, and poets that will find things of interest there. Streets in Srinagar are as hideously dirty as they are in the rest of India. In 2008 there was a news item from Srinagar that caught international attention: that the city was considering mass poisoning an estimated 100,000 population of its stray dogs. (Human population of the city is about 900,000). I do not think that program was carried out, as I found too many dogs. A Kashmiri dog can be found lying prostrate in the middle of a busy street, which moves just enough to let a vehicle or a pedestrian pass by.

Even with having lived life on the sharp blade of a knife in the last two decades, the people are busy living their lives. There is no other way to live life but that way. Kashmiris have shown a lot of resilience, even absorbing silently their self-inflicted wounds. They have changed their history and way of living by their decisions and actions. The common man is fed up with militants, who are a miniscule of the population, who have deep and passionate belief that Kashmiri Muslims do not belong to India. For decades Kashmiris believed that they must join their co-religionist Pakistan, but in the last few years that has changed to becoming an independent nation, insurmountable practical difficulties of which have not sunk deep in their minds. But election after election they have favored the National Conference, a political party which has steadfastly espoused alliance with India over the separatists parties.

As my tour of Srinagar came to an end, I realized that I had only just touched the corners of a flower, its many layers of petals harboring the sites of my childhood and young adulthood had yet to be peeled. I did not visit my high school, the house of my friend Tej Zutshi, walk down the lane which would take me from my house in Malikyar to Habba Kadal and beyond to my college and other places. I did not walk down the road between Habba Kadal and Kralkhud where I was once mistakenly slapped for eve-teasing. I did not go to the Doctors quarters compound in the SMHS Hosptal, where I spent a lot of time playing cricket. I can make amends to this incomplete tour of Srinagar of my childhood by coming to it again.

Not everything is dissolved by the mists of time, some things survive them.

AT THE FEET OF SHIVA AT AMARNATH

After having left Kashmir in 60s to study engineering at Banaras, and not knowing if I was returning back there to work, I was haunted by the lost opportunity to visit Amaranth. Most of the male members of my family and most of my friends had made the trip.

How circumstances had made me be deprived of the visit, I do not remember in detail, but I know my miss was circumstantial. But what is surprising is that I could have kept on harboring my desire to visit Amaranth even over so many decades. What was in it that kept me pulling toward it? Religious ardor? Hiking pleasure? Pull of the stunning natural scenery? I do not know what it was. Like the British mountaineer George Mallory's (1886-1924), (who had made three unsuccessful attempts to climb Mt. Everest), answer, "Because it is there," to the question, "Why do you want to climb Mt. Everest?," I did not have a good explanation for harboring my desire to visit Amarnath for so long, but only my strong feeling to do so.

When I decided to visit Kashmir this August, naturally the thought of visiting Amaranth occurred to me. But I reserved my decision to go there at a later point during the trip, so that I was absolutely certain that I could do so. The reason for doing that was because I had to consider my physical strength at my age to go on high mountains. When I reached Kashmir, within a day I decided that I will go to Amarnath.

On Aug. 10, I got up at 4:00 AM to prepare for the trip to Amarnath. By 5:00 AM I was on the road to Baltal, about 56 miles from Srinagar. It was an eerie feeling to drive at that hour, as the towns and villages were shutdown. In the absence of people places look different; their real personalities come out. How innocent do they look, ready to wear whatever garb humans put them in. Beyond the long strip of the town of Ganderbal, we started encountering the more mountainous terrain. Kangan is a lovely blend of hills, trees, and water, just 25 miles from Srinagar. As we go further beyond this point we start feeling the almost continuous presence of the river Sind: scintillating, spirited, sonorous. What a grace and character it has. River Liddar, flowing in Pahalgam valley, is small and low-key in comparison. On the way we saw some people out of their homes in pre-dawn walks. The silence of the hour puts the walker in a meditative mode. What a good way to start a day in one's life. I could not but see how much simpler is life in villages and towns away from metropolises. Towns of Thajewas and Sonamarg followed.

Driving from Sonamarg, just about 3 to 4 miles from Baltal, the road suddenly turned very rough; it was as yet unpaved road. It was very annoying, as one was close to the significant destination of Baltal, during the *yatra* period, from where the helicopters ferry to Panchtarni, the base-camp of Amarnath. Why cannot the government choose its priorities right?

Baltal is a meadow-like place, with lovely mountainscape. On this sunny morning it looked a forlorn, dreamy place. Within the fenced area of the heliport two companies operate. We were several dozen passengers waiting for our turns to be ferried to Panchtarni. After an hour's wait beyond the schedule, we were carefully seated in the plane. I was accompanied by three ladies and a man in the rear compartment. As the helicopter lifted off, after a usual hiccup, the three ladies got visibly scared and some of them started praying. Within a minute we were smoothly flying. We flew through a mountain pass that seemed very adventurous, especially because the geography was new to me. After five minutes we landed at Panchtarni, the base-camp of the Amaranth cave, which is at an elevation of 12,729 ft.

Panchtarni is valley-like, contoured by dramatically rugged mountains. Like most high mountainscapes, it has the aura of otherworldliness, the mood of renunciation. I felt I could live here for a while: to meditate on a spirit higher than that is manifest to us through senses.

I decided to go on a horseback to the cave rather than walk, considering my aging frame.

Amnarnath cave is only about four miles from Panchtarni but the road is fraught with high steep. If that were not enough hardship, the road is just a few feet wide, wildly meandering at places, unpaved, and strewn quite often with huge rocks. And there are ravines thousands of feet below to scare you. In U.S. such a route would be impermissible for mass travel for safety reasons. Why would the government not make this heavily trafficked road safe? It would not need any foreign technology to do that, just rupees, planning, and effort.

My trek started smoothly, fuelled as it was with high motivation. But as I climbed higher into the folds of the mountains, my leg bones started to pain. But I am not an easy quitter. I have many times ruined my projects by not quitting early enough; I am a prisoner of my will. As I moved on with the caravan of *yatris,* I started thinking of how people undertake this arduous and expensive journey. Many of the *yatris* I saw were old, much older than I am, and also seemed to be of modest financial means. What gave them the strength to first embark on this journey? It was not much difficult for me to understand that it was their faith in God that propelled them.

As we climbed higher into the mountain my legs became sore and I started thinking of what to do. I could walk, perhaps relieving pressure on my legs, or I could tell my horseman to look into the saddle straps and stirrups, as their faulty set up might be the culprit. But I did not convert these ideas into actions, for reasons unknown to me. Insane that it was, I just kept on going like the soldiers in the poem *The Charge Of The Light Brigade,* whose mission was dictated by the order: *Theirs is not to reason why/Theirs is but to do and die.* Sometimes I looked at the very old woman in our group, whose back was doubled up; I wondered how she was coping with the journey. But because she was ahead of me and so I was unable to see her face, I could not tell. There were other *yatris*, who were older than I am, but none appeared to be in pain. I knew, with the utmost confidence of my being, that the cancellation of the trip was not an option I had. Remembering that in other similar situations, when I was under intense pressure to continue on a path because I was in utter discomfort, I had kept on. This faith in myself propelled me ahead in my present calamity.

The scenery on the way is mystic and tranquilizing; you feel you are far away from the world. You are solely focused on the journey and its destination. Those who are religious must be thinking of God, those who believe in the mystery and power of nature think of it. They are two different ways for humans to live in harmony with themselves and the outside world. Such journeys as we were undertaking unconsciously detach you from yourself and make you think of some reality higher than that. Living in the survival struggle, unfairness, and coldness of the world, compels most of the people to find the security in one's self. That leads to the creation of ego, which then becomes a vicious black-hole, from where the escape becomes an extraordinarily difficult task. If the world were different, as it has been at times in the history of mankind, human beings would live more peacefully than they do now. Today's *maya jaal* is a tough prison, braced as it is with heavy materialism and its inhuman sister, technology.

The thinker in me could not avoid, although I tried my utmost not to think on the subject, thinking about why people undertake an arduous and an expensive journey to Amaranth. There were many very old men and women, physically decrepit, for whom the journey was hazardous. What is this force, this compulsion, which pulled them to Amarnath? Since the birth of man in the cosmos he has been seeking the ultimate reality; as if his very birth involved the separation from it so that he was compelled to reunite with it. This eternal longing of man to be with God is the very fabric of life, the essence of human existence, the driving force of the propagation of human soul. Man wants to be reunited with the flame that in the first place propelled him into the journey through the world. Why did gods create this puzzling game? We do not know, but in the absence of our understanding of it, we have to assume that they had a good reason for it.

The horses we were riding on were of small build but were tough. They knew their job very well. In many situations, when there was more than one path available to negotiate, from a human intelligence point of view, all horses would follow the same path. They were very dexterous in negotiating complex maneuvers; for example, when climbing up and down a rock. When a horse appeared to be slackening in his efforts, the horseman would admonish it with a particular noise, *frrah,* and the horse would react with the expected improvement in its performance.

The cave is on the other side of the mountain from which one starts at Panchtarni. So, when you turn the side of the mountain, the emotion to have Shiva's *darshan* rises. Also, the trek on the other side is milder. The closer you get to the cave, the lower does the altitude of the road gets. For those who are on a maiden journey, the emotions for *darshan* are accompanied with curiosity and the possibilities of surprises. Reaching the last mile to the destination the crescendo of emotions rises perceptibly. Finally, you reach Amarnath, but are crestfallen to learn that you have still some more journeying to do to reach the cave. There are about 70 steps on a steep incline to climb to get into the Amarnath cave. My leg pain seemed to vanish, except that its shadow reverberated in the memory. I thought I needed a moment of respite before the final push to *darshan.* I went into a tented *daaba* and slaked my thirst and hunger by drinking tea and devouring some snacks. While still eating I learnt that the place was a charity operation. I could not but feel admiration for those contributing money and efforts for it; the world was not, after all, completely insensitive.

After nourishing and resting the beaten body a little, I strode on toward the steps. Right before going over the first of them I took a look at the cave. It seemed larger than it had appeared in the pictures; maybe, because of the three-dimensionality of the view. The largeness of the mouth of the cave portended that it might be very deep as well, an abbreviated cosmos of spirituality. At this point in my journey the mystery of Amaranth burned scintillatingly in my mind, the prospect of being in the cave shortly quickened my breath. I was very surprised to see that I too wanted to have a *darshan.* I realized that aren't we all human beings searchers of something larger than our existences, something more beautiful than our environments.

The fierce ruggedness of Mt. Amarnath and its companion mountains seemed to be in sharp contrast with the spiritual light enshrined there. Were the mountains protecting something sensitive and inestimable? The legend that Lord Shiva revealed to his consort Parvati the secrets of life and eternity in the cave flashed across my mind. I felt that was an awesome place he had chosen for such an awesome revelation.

But the climbing of the steps became painful, because of their steepness and because of the accumulated tiredness of the journey already made. Even young people, some of whom looked less than half my age, were taking breathers every ten steps climbed. This observation made me feel less critical of my self-control.

Finally, I entered the cave, in a line of *yatris.* The first impression was that its depth was shallow, about 20 ft., compared to its outside width and height of about 45 and 150 ft. There was plenty of time to be inside the cave as at this time of close to the end of the *yatra* there were only a few hundred *yatris.* There was no *darshan,* which was not unexpected for this time of the year. I was told that in June there was a full 16 ft. *darshan.* There is a popular theory floating around that the military helicopter traffic near the cave had raised the temperatures in the cave, resulting in the early disappearance of the *darshan.* But I was not disappointed by the lack of *darshan,* as it was not its physical presence that was necessary for my mind to appreciate its significance. For me it is the legend of Amarnath that is so captivating, not its scientific authenticity, because it signifies to me the eternal human thirst for truth, beauty, and knowledge. I spent fifteen minutes looking at the wall in the cave where Shiva's, Parvati's, and their son Ganesha's *lingums* usually stand. I imagined the millions of people, who over centuries have visited the cave to find their salvation. I was moved by this human yearning to find the release from the bondages of the flesh and the shackles of the world. I could not help thinking the great irony of man's life: though one of the supreme creations in the universe, he is in pain throughout his stay in the world, the release from which he so ardently seeks.

After having *darshan* the mood of satisfaction invisibly penetrated me. I was no longer thinking but felt to be in a benign daze; as if submerged in a deep lake, from which I did not want to be disturbed for awhile.

After taking *prasad* and resting a little the return trip to Panchtarni started. A mood of bathos slowly descended. The return journey was easier but yet strenuous, as the same elements of the narrowness of the road, punctuated with huge rocks, and extreme steepness existed as in the other direction. Slowly and surely we trekked to Panchtarni, a dreamy valley, laced with beautifully rugged mountains, reminding one of eternity.

From Panchtarni we travelled back to Baltal by a helicopter. From there on I boarded my waiting taxi. We stopped at the town of Sonamarg: a place of almost absolute tranquility, pregnant with a mystic mood, transporting one to a different cosmos.

After following the dancing rhythms of the whitewater river Sind for quite a while, we reentered the civilization. Passing through the hamlets, villages, and little towns once again impressed on me the superiority of living close to nature.

Reaching my hotel in Srinagar, I felt that I had still not been able to lift the corner of the veil of mystery over my lifelong urge to visit Amaranth.

ARTICLES
ON KASHMIRIS

MEETING RAJ BEGUM

(November 29, 2011)

I had a great opportunity to meet Kashmir's legendary singer Raj Begum in August, 2011.

Meeting Raj Begum

It was sometime in early 70s when I was paddling through the back waters of my life that I realized that I liked Raj Begum's singing very much. It was her deep drilling haunting voice that captured my imagination. There were other good singers but none had the sorrowful, almost a mournful, and poignant voice that Raj Begum had.

I used to listen to her occasionally on radio when I lived in Kashmir, but now I wanted to listen to her extensively. But where to get her music, as it was not sold anywhere? So, I started the search for Raj Begum's music, which lasted over several years.

On my three different visits to India in 70s, I met different people in Srinagar, who I thought might help me obtain Raj Begum's music. In one of the trips I carried a bottle of Johnnie Walker whiskey from U.S. to be used as a bribe to get my goodies. But even that failed to do the job, as in the all the cases I would be given a cassette of her music, which when played back home in New York, would deliver at the most one or two of her songs. I was frustrated and disheartened and was about to throw in my towel. But before I did so an idea flashed to me: why don't I write to my uncle, who until recently used to hold an I.G.P's position in the Jammu and Kashmir government. The rationale was that because of his high-level position his network of contacts ought to deliver the cat. I wrote to him in 1988 and lo and behold within two months I had a cassette filled with 93 minutes of songs of Raj Begum. I was ecstatic beyond ordinary experience; an inner joy seemed to glow through my mind.

At the heel of this stunning success, within a year a relative travelling from India on a business visit to New York met me. He worked for All India Radio, New Delhi, but previously had worked for Radio Kashmir, in Srinagar. I told him that by virtue of his connections with his previous posting, he ought to be able to get more of Raj Begum's music for me, as obviously the great singer had sung many hundreds of songs. My relative felt challenged, especially because my uncle, who was his relative too, had an achievement to his credit in this field. My relative accepted the challenge and I handed him the highest quality cassette I could buy. But, in spite of his bravado to accept the challenge, I had doubts about his ability to deliver the goods; the reason being that he was a very busy bureaucrat. But a miracle did happen, as within six weeks I got another 80 minutes of songs of Raj Begum.

Now I possessed 2 hours and 45 minutes of songs of Raj Begum; so I was in the company of a select group of lucky people. People measure their fortunes in money, but I measured it by the number of Raj Begum's songs that I possessed.

I made many copies of my booty and generously gave it away to my friends. But I realized that every Kashmiri should have access to all of Raj Begum's music, which was much more than 2 hours and 45 minutes of songs, but which was not available, because of a special situation. When Raj Begum started singing professionally, in mid-50s, only radio stations had recording equipment. Her best years of singing were spent working for Radio Kashmir, with the result that her entire music is only available through it. Having the mentality of a Government of India department, Radio Kashmir did not think it was their business to release a singer's music, even if the singer was of as high a caliber and legendary as Raj Begum was.

So, I launched a project to make Raj Begum's music accessible to people. I sought the help of my friend Kailash Mehra, a renowned Kashmiri singer. She approached a deputy director of Radio Kashmir about the project but met discouragement. I thought of getting the help of Farooq Abdullah, a former chief minister of Jammu and Kashmir, and now a central government minister, who is an ardent lover and supporter of Kashmir music. But this also fizzled out due to practical difficulties.

In 2011 I had an awesome chance to speak to the director Radio Kashmir and meet Raj Begum, as I went on a trip to Kashmir in August. It looked like too good to be true. But I had to try to achieve both the items to the best of my abilities. Due to Kailash Mehra's help I met Rehmatullah Khan, a well-known singer and a senior artist of Radio Kashmir, and the son of the renowned music composer Nassarullah Khan. He arranged my meetings with Raj Begum and the director of Radio Kashmir.

I waited with an excited expectation and keen eagerness for Raj Begum's arrival for lunch outside Shamiyana restaurant, at Dal Gate, Srinagar, on August 13. Almost exactly at 2:00 P.M. she arrived in an auto-rickshaw. She stepped out of the auto with measured though delicate steps. I approached her with joyful trepidation. She waited for me to come to her and though standing toward me she seemed to be looking at nothing. She was of small of build, slim, and composed. Her face was age-beaten but poised. She seemed to have seen a million tragedies but having refused to be blown off the ground. A patina of time skinned her face. With a torrent of thoughts gushing through me I just managed to greet her. She reciprocated with a dignified movement of her body. A young man escorting her I was later told was her grandson Irshad Lone. Soon Rehmatullah Khann joined us. Getting into the restaurant we were told, in a comic turn of the event, that it was closed for the afternoon due to some reason.

We went to another restaurant at Dal Gate, just a half-mile away. We started talking about the old times, 50s and 60s. Raj Begum recited many names in the music world of that era. When I asked her if Farooq Abdullah was an ardent lover of Kashmiri music, she replied that Bakshi Gulam Mohammed was much more so. Soon Rehmatullah told her that it would be a good idea for her to record some songs for me. I was taken aback by it as I had never thought of that. To my utter surprise she excitedly agreed to it. Now Rehmatullah started discussing with her which should be the ten songs she would sing. At this a burst of enthusiasm took hold of her. She started humming lines of songs. The meeting lasted an hour.

The first day of recording was set for August 19 at Zee Studio, at Residency Road. She was escorted this time by her son Mohammad Ramzan. Rehmatullah and she started going through the motions of setting up the tunes of the songs. She sang in a deliberate, though practiced, manner. Her song-laden voice came from deep within her, her hand-gesturing only giving it an after-delivery confirmation. Her delivery was smooth, without an apparent effort. She seemed not to need much musical instrument support for her singing. Here I was seeing the performance of the greatest Kashmiri singer that I knew of. It was an ecstatically dramatic moment for me. What more did I want in life, I thought?

During the recording break I engaged her in a conversation. I asked her at what age did she tell her family that she was going to be a professional singer. She told me that it was 21. I asked her this question because in the days of her youth singing was considered to be a low-level profession, more so for women, who would be taken to be of low moral caliber. I further asked her what difficulties she faced in the society because of her profession. She told me that her husband forbade her to sing publically. But after a show of rage about it he let her sing. She also told me that the renowned *ghazal* singer Begum Akhtar told her to switch to *ghazal* singing.

Further conversation with her elicited that though she had been bestowed a thousand awards but was hardly rewarded monetarily. I learned furthermore from other sources that she was poor, as the sole source of her income before her retirement had been the Radio Kashmir salary, which is so meager that it is a cruel joke. Here we have the greatest singer of Kashmir having difficulty making two ends meet. In Kashmir artists do not amount to much in public estimation. They cannot make a living on their artistic work. Any nation that does not value their artists is a backward nation, as art uplifts the human soul equal in caliber to religion.

At the end of the first recording session she told me that she was going to resume her daily *riyaaz*. Obviously, meeting an ardent admirer of hers and recording her songs after an absence of some six years she was exultant, which gave a boost to her musical soul.

Next in line for me was to meet the director of Radio Kashmir Mr.Javied Iqbal. I explained to him why recordings of Raj Begum had to be made available to the public because (a) they were not available commercially and (b) because she was an outstanding artist, whose work brought joy to Kashmiris, especially the ones living in the countries far away from India, who would get home-sick easily. I told the director that the recordings should be released to me, so that I could inform the world-wide Kashmiri community of their availability, a task I presumed Radio Kashmir would not like to do itself. Any proceeds from the distribution of her music would be given to Radio Kashmir. In fact, I suggested that they should be rather given to Raj Begum, in light of her strained economic conditions. In case Radio Kashmir did not want to give me the recordings, they should make them available on a website. I told the director that diffusion and continuation of Kashmiri music such as Raj Begum's songs must be a mission for Radio Kashmir, which is a preservation of the best of Kashmiri culture. He seemed to understand my points very well, and in that direction asked me to give him a letter stating my case. Which was eminently understandable to me in light of Indian government's bureaucracy's deep penchant for paperwork. Two days later the memorandum was delivered to him. Weeks melted into months, there was no response. At one point Rehmatullah indicated to me that based on some brief conversation he had with the director it seemed that the matter would be decided in my favor. But this good news did not convert to an official decision. When my friend again inquired about it, the director told him that he had already "released" Raj Begum's previously recorded music, and since she did not professionally sing anymore he did not have to release anything. This statement was incomprehensible to me because if Raj Begum's music had been released to the public, why wasn't it available anywhere? It was an absurd statement made just to get out of the trap he found himself in. He didn't have the decency to even reply to my letter. What killed my project was sheer Indian bureaucratic arrogance. So, Raj Begum's music lies buried in the Radio Kashmir archives forever. So much love Kashmiris have for the arts and artists.

The second session of the recording on August 22 for the CD dedicated to me had to be cancelled on account of Raj Begum's sickness. On August 23 I had to return to Delhi. Later on the recording was completed and the CD is now in its cover design stage. I have called the CD *Songs From The Corners Of My Heart.*

Raj Begum was born in a poor family of Magarbal Bagh, Srinagar, on March 27, 1927. Her father was Ghulam Rasool Sheikh. Like most of the great singers she started singing in her childhood. As she grew up she sang in marriage parties. It is only later in her life she received some formal training in singing, which came from the established musicians like Ustad Jhandee Khan, Ustad Muhammad Abdullah Tibetbakal, Ustad Muhammad Qaleenbaaf, and others.

Raj Begum was introduced to Radio Kashmir, Srinagar by the well-known folk singer Ghulam Qadir Langoo. She started her career there on July 16, 1954. Her unique voice and delivery of songs drew the attention of music lovers right away, especially her rendering of the famous love tale *Gulrez.* She went on to sing at Radio Kashmir till 1986.

She has sung in most of the genres of singing: folk, religious, *ghazals*, romantic, light, etc. It is difficult to estimate the number of songs she has sung as in the early days of Radio Kashmir it did not have recording equipment; a singer sang live. Often no records were kept. Some people familiar with the Kashmiri music scene estimate that she has sung a few thousand songs. Besides my estimation of Raj Begum to be the greatest Kashmiri singer of the modern times, it is also the popular opinion. The following songs of her have entered the Kashmiri folklore:

- *Vyasiye gulan aavuy bahar*
- *Subuh phul bulbulav tul shore-googa*
- *Rum ghayam sheeshas byegur gov baane myon*
- *Wal az vyasiye dokh sukh mashrith sherawloluk bagh*
- *Kyah roze pardan chaaye chaaye soze-jigar myon*

She had the courage to break the social stigma of women singing in public, when she along with another great Kashmiri singer Naseem Akhtar, went to sing for Radio Kashmir. She was married to Qadir Ganderbali, who was a D.I.G. Police with the Jammu And Kashmir State when he passed away several years ago. She lives at Channapora, Srinagar.

Some of the notable awards she has won:

- Sadiq Memorial Award
- Robe Of Honor from Jammu And Kashmir Academy Of Art, Culture, And Languages
- Gold Medal For Best Concert In Kashmiri Folk Music by Jammu And Kashmir State
- Silver Shield by Kala Kendra
- Bakshi Memorial Committee award
- Certificate Of Excellence from Prasar Bharti (1999)
- Government Of Madhya Pradesh State Award (2004)
- Jammu And Kashmir State Excellence In Folk Music (2008)
- Jammu and Kashmir State Cultural Award Winner (Golden Jubilee, 2009)
- Padma Shri (2002)

Since returning to New York I have been regularly in touch with her either directly or through her family members. She recently underwent a gall bladder removal surgery and seems to be recuperating well. Next year when I return to Kashmir I plan to meet her again, as she is as precious to me as Dal Lake is.

Sat Lal Razdan

A Ray Of Light Through The Darkness

(October 20, 2009)

Sat Lal Razdan was a great teacher, who by his talent, imagination, and ambition made a lasting impact on the students of Biscoe School in Srinagar and the education system in the State Of Jammu and Kashmir, from 1947 thru 1988.

Sat Lal Razdan

A Ray Of Light Through The Darkness

When we think of Sat Lal Razdan we think of a high level teacher who shaped the character and career of a few generations of students in Jammu and Kashmir State. He was original and innovative in his teaching approach and uncompromisable in his work. Add to that the ambition and energy he brought to his work. Anyone taught by Sat Lal Razdan for a reasonable length of time would not remain the same as he was before that. As the biannual anniversary of his passing away on April 29th is approaching we again mourn the loss of this brilliant teacher. If we only had a few dozen teachers like Sat Lal Razdan the modern history of Kashmir in some areas might have been different than it has been.

Master Sat Lal, as students used to call him fondly, was born on 6th June, in 1924, at Anantnag, Kashmir. He passed his matriculation from Mission School, Anantnag. He was awarded "The best all-round boy" by Tyndale Biscoe in 1941. He graduated with distinction from Government College, Lahore, then considered at the level of Oxford University, in 1945, majoring in science. Later on he attended Prince Of Wales College in Jammu for bachelor's in teaching. In 1947 he was appointed a master in Tyndale Biscoe School, in Srinagar. He went on to be in that institution till 1984, rising up to the level of headmaster. Immediately after that term he was reemployed by the school till 1988. Overall he spent 41 years in Biscoe School.

In 40's and earlier the cultural and social environment in Kashmir was vastly different from what it is today. In fact the difference is so enormous that it is hard to believe it. The aim of the education then for the students and their parents was to just pass the examinations so as to get jobs in the government. Extra-curricular activities were shunned because they detracted the time from the education and were also culturally looked down upon, especially by Pandits. Preconceived notions from religion strongly influenced the development of a student's personality. The pursuit of knowledge was a flimsy goal, as a student believed all his knowledge came from his religion. Students were docile, diffident, and meek. There was very little idealism in the society. Survival was the prime focus of nearly all the efforts a man expended.

The Misson School, the forerunner of Tyndale Biscoe School, was started around 1881 by Rev. J.H. Knowles. Students attended it to learn English as that was replacing Persian in certain state offices. Soon the foreign school staff learned the tremendous barriers that they had to cross to impart modern education to Kashmiri students. It was indeed a heroic struggle for the school to soften some of those barriers. This school has had a tremendous impact on the development of the modern Kashmiri education and culture. Kashmiri students did not want to play games, go hiking, or swim. They only wanted to learn in the classrooms. The school carried the European vision of sports being a necessary activity to develop a person's character, his sense of enterprise, and the worldly competitiveness. It is hard to believe that in a place of lakes, rivers, and ponds people did not like to learn swimming. Athletics in general were offensive to Kashmiris. If a house was burning or men were drowning people would crowd around the accident scene to watch an extraordinary happening but not lend rescue efforts. The Mission School went all the way to inculcate a sense of civic duty among its students. So that in the ending part of the 19th Century its students would help rescue people in fires and floods, and help people during cholera epidemics that would visit Kashmir often those times. So, for Mission School teachers education meant more than book learning, it meant being an active person who engaged in sports, hiking, and in social calamities where he could be of help. Even in learning they preached a different doctrine. They believed that a person grasp the practical aspects of a subject besides any esoteric aspects it might have. They were against learning by rote, which was then the Kashmiri approach to learning. The Biscoe School's motto *In All Things Be Men* bears an excellent summary of its educational philosophy. By "men" is meant people who combine both the values of strength and kindness. The school crest consists of two rowing paddles with heart shaped blades crossing each other with the motto encircling them. The paddles indicate hard work and strength and the heart shaped blades symbolize kindness. The crossing of the paddles express sacrifice and Christian cross.

The well established Mission School philosophy of education was the environment which Sat Lal encountered when he joined Biscoe School in 1947. He was familiar with it to an extent as he had studied earlier in Mission School, Anantnag. But Sat Lal imparted his own personality and imagination to the philosophy and teaching of the school. His activist approach to teaching, in and off the class room, was more than ordinary. He seemed to have thought that education is something like the air we breathe in–it is needed every time. He made sure that his students were well-versed in the local geography, current affairs, and other general knowledge. Even though general knowledge was not covered by exams but he believed it was essential for an educated man. I do not know how many teachers in his day thought like him or thought so vigorously about it as he thought. Even though having general knowledge was an extension of Mission School philosophy but in the hands of Sat Lal it became an indispensable requirement for a student to have. Sat Lal had become so famous a teacher in his time that many politically well connected and wealthy families hired him to teach their children, so that they would do well in exams. Also, hiring Sat Lal had become a social status. He taught many people who rose to high positions in the government and commerce. But the families' power and wealth did not deter him to be as hard with their children as he thought was necessary to educate them. His toughness was a salient feature of his character.

Sat Lal's communication and rapport with his students was special and it became a great asset to him in educating them. A teacher's personality, at a school level education, is of greater value than even his knowledge of the subject he is teaching. A teacher or a leader influences his audience by touching their sensitive points. Students want their teacher to be good looking, well poised, respectful to them, articulate, un-stiff, and in command of the subject he is teaching. Sat Lal possessed all these qualities and some more.

Sat Lal possessed a larger than life image which elevated him to become a great teacher. Also, he would generally know the weak and the strong points of his students and he used that knowledge to lift their academic and personality levels. His authoritativeness was well balanced with his humor, courteousness, tact, chutzpah, and sheer enthusiasm for his work.

Where did Sat Lal's vision of education come from? A good part of it came from Mission School education philosophy but why were not other teachers in Biscoe School as successful as he was. So, the factors of his success partially stemmed from beyond the school. We have to search for them in his upbringing, education, and personality. Human mind is a vast mosaic which grows and changes. While I do not have good knowledge of Sat Lal's mental history but it seems to me his personality had a large role to play in his teaching abilities. Obviously, he believed education to be a mind stretcher. That is, the quality of a mind grows when it is taught to do things as against when it just memorizes them. Perhaps, Master Sat Lal would agree with what the renowned American jurist, Oliver Wendell Holmes, thought: "Man's mind stretched to a new idea never goes back to its original dimensions." Teaching how to live life would be the greatest education we could have but the mankind does not yet know how to do that but teaching a student how to think is obviously of very great value. So, to acquire the knowledge of the standard subjects with an ability to think about them has to be the aim of all school education. We hope later this ability could mature to help a person to live a good life.

With time Sat Lal's renown rose and his recognition followed. The British Council chose him for training in Scotland for full term in 1964.He was awarded "Best teacher Of The Millennium" in 1999 by the Tyandale and Mallinson Education Society. In 2002 he was awarded "Dr. Yog Prakash Award" by D.B.N. School, Jammu. He wrote a book, "Science And Spirit" in 2000 which was well liked.

It is very difficult to estimate the impact of an outstanding teacher like Sat Lal Razdan on a society in certain time period but we can say that he inspired many a student he taught. At his passing away one of his old pupils, Dr. Farooq Abdullah, the former chief minister Of Jammu & Kashmir state, travelled from Srinagar to Jammu to attend his funeral. The present chief minister, Omar Abdullah, had his office make a statement on his passing away. His name is enshrined in the hearts and minds of the students he taught and the people who knew about his contributions to the Kashmiri society, and in the history of Mission and Biscoe Schools. Besides missing a beloved teacher we miss a man of warmth and charm.

> Like a ray of light in darkness
> He wanted to remove one world
> And replace it with another–
> To awaken a new consciousness,
> And ignite a new spirit.

THE LATA MANGESHKAR OF KASHMIR SINGS IN NEW YORK

This article was written on Kailash Mehra Sadhu's concert in New York on August 28, 2003.

THE LATA MANGESHKAR OF
KASHMIR SINGS IN NEW YORK

When it was all over after four hours of singing, Kailash Mehra's concert was giddying, dazzling, and enchanting–transporting us to old Kashmir of our forefathers and our childhoods, which lies now forlornly dead.

The power of Kailash Mehra's singing lies in its enormous range, texture, variety, and nuance. She is truly Kashmir's Lata Mangeshkar. Though of a small build Kailash Ji can produce a voice that is booming and towering, if the song demands it be so. Just by listening to one concert of hers one gets an idea of her long immersion in music–training as well as experience. She sang the immortal folk songs, popular songs, and meditative songs. She even threw a couple of *ghazals,* showing us that she could have had the whole concert in that genre of singing. But it were the folk songs that drilled through our hearts by their universality, simplicity, and haunting melody.

How is that this lady who was born in U.P. in a Punjabi family has come to become a doyen of Kashmiri singing. Her family came from Sailkot (now in Pakistan) and when she was just in single-digit years of age it moved to Kashmir. She grew up, went to school and college there. She stayed in Kashmir till 1989 when the war broke, forcing her to move to Jammu. To be as accomplished a singer as Kailash Ji is a person has to be very gifted. Singing at higher levels is not just being endowed with a good singing apparatus and having a good training but it takes a keenness of mind to feel the nuances of the culture a singer is singing in. To be able to sing the folk songs of Kashmir the way Kailash Ji sings, she had to absorb Kashmiri culture. Getting to know her while she was staying with us, I could see the depth of her penetration in Kashmiri culture. Also I came to see the other aspects of her personality. She has the sense and the sensibility of an artist. Her sensitivity to people, her sentimentality, her connection with the distant past, and her awe for the established outstanding singers and singing in general was quite apparent. She has been singing for some four decades, since she was a child. (Singers are most generally discovered while they are children) She is a living legend in Jammu and Kashmir and yet she carries herself in awesome and magical humility. I was touched by her humanness, easy affability, and humility. To have crossed from her birth-culture to another culture and excelled so well in it is itself a sign of originality and force of personality.

Kailash Mehra Sadhu's concert in Tri-state area (New York, Connecticut, New Jersey) and northern Pennsylvania was held in Clarkstown Senior High School, West Nyack, New York under the auspices of K.O.A. It was the only place where an auditorium was used for her concert in her U.S. tour. (I do not know what kind of hall was used in Toronto, Canada concert). The acoustics of the auditorium accompanied by the sound system provided by Kalpesh Patel created an exceedingly pleasing musical environment. To this if we add the superb *tabla* playing by Dharmendar Tapodhan (this was the opinion of Kailash Ji) and excellent synthesizer playing by Vijoo Jacob, a music listener's dream came true. Kailash Ji was ecstatic about these physical attributes of her concert. We had an almost four hours of undiluted and unvarnished experience of a sublime and superb singing. Kailash Ji's performance was smooth, polished, versatile, and deliberate. The choice of her songs filled an entire gamut of Kashmiri culture, from folk to *bjajans.* She generously catered to a long string of *farmish.*

The concert ended with a session of thank-you's and the award of a plaque from K.O.A. president Sanjay Kaul (who was on hand to assure that he took Kailash Ji the following day to perform in Boston Concert)

The sublimity of the concert was followed by a delicious Kashmiri dinner catered by Jewel Of India (Manager: Rattan Lal Koul)

Many of the ninety-three concert attendees at the end felt that $40 apiece concert admission was not a high price to pay for the quality of the evening they experienced.

Long after the concert's visible signs faded, its glow has lingered on in some attendee's minds. Here was this evening when with the magic of Kailash Mehra's singing they were immersed in a culture which has given us our identity and roots–two of the most powerful forces in a man's life. We are physically apart from Kashmir but the concert reminded us that actually Kashmir lives on silently in our hearts. Like an angel Kailash Ji came to liberate us from our fetters for a short time but this fleeting freedom seemed eternal while we were listening to her singing. She showed us that paradises are not always far away and out of our abilities to get them, they can be summoned by gifted people to enchant us, howsoever briefly.

POEMS ON KASHMIR

All the poems presented here have been written after the inception of the civil war in Kashmir in 1989; they bear the pain of the suffering it has caused, longing to be there, and nostalgia for the life lived there.

WE HAVE A RENDEZVOUS
WITH DESTINY

Written For The 1ˢᵗ Kashmiri Pandit Youth Conference
To Be Held At Pune, India On January 7 & 8, 2012

Let the word go forth from Pune that a new generation of Kashmiri youth
Has embarked on a mission to excel in management and business, science and technology,
They will show the world how to be high-achievers with hard work and humility, grace and peace,
They have written their will in the stars and have set up a rendezvous with destiny.

With the head held high and the heart glowing strong,
Our youth in Pune assemble in an august conference,
To galvanized their resolve to take charge of their future,
To be the shining stars of our community and leaders of our nation.

Much is expected of our youth, as much has been given to them.
They are the children of Vitasta, the continuation of Harmukh,
They are the blessings of Khirbavani and the eternal peace of Amarnath,
They are the light that has gathered over Kashmiri Pandits over thousands of years.

Maharaj Kaul

Our children are ready to walk
The path their fathers and forefathers travelled on,
They are ready to honor our roots and ethos,
The world has changed a lot since the first Pandit
Walked the hallowed ground in Kashmir 5,000 years ago.

For thousands of years we kept burning our flame
At the altar of learning and righteous creed,
Today we have been castigated from our ancestral home,
Strewn carelessly over the crust of the earth,
Scrambling for our identity and roots.

But today is the day of celebration for our youth,
Today is the day of rejoicing for our community,
We look to our future with confidence and joy
And feel our youth will carry our flag forward

I HAVE COME TO SEE YOU, MOTHER

I am at the Dal Lake shore,
Wanting to put a garland round your neck,
I have come to see you, Mother,
Friends beseeched me not to visit you,
As there were many militants hiding in your folds,
Waiting to harm visitors, to be on the headlines,
To bring attention to their cause,
To pry justice from the "occupying" country.

Kasheer, the footprint of my life,
The cradle of my being,
Here I formed the first atoms of my consciousness,
Dreamt the first unpretentious dream,
Had the first rounds of my battles with the world,
Suffered the first heartbreak.

But I could not care less for the blood-drenched anarchists,
Who want to turn *Kasheer* into a theocracy,
Catering essentially to one faith,
But being unfaithful to democracy,
They have written their will across the stars,
But here on earth they fight dirty in the trenches,
I could not but come to see you Mother,
It is beyond politics, fear, and rationality.

There are two *Kasheers:*

225

Maharaj Kaul

One in the mountains, meadows, and lakes,
The other in the cities, towns, and villages where people live,
There are two faiths that are available here:
One preaches peace, beauty, and equality,
The other: war, hatred, and insanity.
It is a duel between God and man,
Who will win any fool can answer.

I am not interested in man's follies and lust,
I want to touch the corner of time,
I want to be an element of universe,
I love not man less,
But I trust nature more,
My umbilical cord with *Maej Kasheer,*
Pulls me to her, unmindful of fear and sneer.

I went to Shalimar, Nishat, and Chashma Shahi,
I skimmed on Dal Lake endlessly,
And saw fish and lotuses pink and yellow,
And their round green shawls,
They greeted me with pregnant silences,
They wanted to say a lot to me but the lack of privacy hindered.

In Pahalgam there is a thin veil of a stream,
Streaming vigorously in spite of the boulders trying to impede it,
Liddar has frothed and frolicked for a thousand years,
Defying the authority and foolishness of man,
The ring of the mountains with choreographed undulations
Circle Liddar with easy majesty,
The utterly graceful pine trees dot them in an ethereal needlepoint
design,
Unmindful of the flow of time.

Have you seen the different moods of Dal Lake:
Scintillating, serene, sublime, sad, saucy,
We think we understand her but the foolishness of that claim

Is apparent to anyone knowing even a little,
Man makes big of his understanding and achievements,
Talents and unquestioned authority,
But gods laugh at his littleness and silliness,
And do not know where to begin removing the veil of ignorance over him.

In Zethyar I apologized to Shesta Devi for coming to her for the first time,
She eyed me with a compelling serenity that sent shivers down my spine,
I was reminded of my sinful past and irresolute stance to do better in future,
I lingered in the compound yearning to have a spiritual outlook,
But my reverie was broken by the thought that even sinners can find life valuable,
If they are truthful, work hard, and keep their mouth shut.

The meadow of Gulmarg looks to be a transition to something heavenly,
What has man done to embellish it, nothing, but scattered a cluster of hotels?
The central part of Gulmarg, its face, is so natural that it lacks any worldly sophistication,
An incredible opportunity to adorn it has been squandered,
Under the starry-skies of Gulmarg one feels that God is eavesdropping,
Happiness is a worldly concept,
Pine-suffused mountains of Gulmarg create an aura beyond happiness.

Nowhere in the mist over Dal Lake is written *Azadi*,
As Dal Lake is eternally free, no one can imprison it,
Without inner freedom there can be no outer freedom,
Freedom is a state of mind, not a political contract or a religious ecstasy,
God is freedom, to be contemplated, meditated on, and lived,

Man was born free but politics and organized religions have chained him,
Let's break these chains, we have nothing to lose but our sorrows.

In the folds of Kashmir mountains resides the solemnity of gods,
In the swirls of its breezes plays the music of the universe,
Kashmir is the eternal enigmatic smile of God,
Disturbed now by some selfish and rude outsiders and insiders,
A dagger thrust in the grand design,
My tears flow to wash its wounds.

Today I have snuffed out all my fears,
Trampled all the taboos,
Discarded all the customs,
Broken all the worldly chains,
I have come to see *Kasheer,* my Mother.

WE WILL MARCH ON AND ON

We march on and on toward our motherland,
They may break our bones, they may hate us,
But our resolve to reclaim our land is written in the stars.

We were born 5,000 years ago in *Kasheer*,
We grew up on the knees of the high mountain peaks and the
transparent lakes,
Caressed by cool breezes and hugged by flower meadows,
We were nurtured by Buddhism and Shaivism.

We are the spirit of Shiva and children of Vitasta,
We are blessed by Khirbhavani and we are protected by Durga,
They can destroy our homes, they can neglect out shrines,
But they cannot break our spirits to reclaim our land,
We march on and on.

They may expel us from the Valley but the Valley lives in us,
We have a rendezvous with destiny,
We will march on and on till we return to our land.

THE MIRACLE OF
MAHARAJNI KHIR BHAVANI

She sits in immense grandeur in the Tulmul *nag* island temple,
Presiding over the protection and well being of Kashmiris:
She is Maharajni Khir Bhavani, Kashmir's supreme and the
newest goddess.
She is also called Tripurasundri, Shyama, Rajni, Ragniya;
She has held at various times aspects also of Kali and Sita.
Her prophecies of the state of life in Kashmir are rendered by the
color of the water in the *nag*.
She is a Tantaric goddess, a vegetarian and a virgin,
She is worshipped by Shiva and Rama.

Over time her iconic image has changed in some ways
But in a classic one she is seated in a yogic *asna* on a thousand
petal lotus bedecked hexagonal seat
Wearing a bejeweled crown,
She has a third eye in the middle of her forehead and she has four
arms:
Upper right carries a lotus, left a spear; lower right a poison/elixir
container, left an auspicious vessel;
She is flanked by Vishnu on the right and Shiva on the left.
A supreme *Tantaric* goddess equipped with powerful cultic
paraphernalia.

Her *murti, mantra,* and *yantra* are for people to understand and
worship,

And realize what they want.

Her fifteen syllable *mantra* is:

Aum, Hrim, Shrim, Ram, Klim, Sau, Bhagavatyai, Rajnyai, Hrim, Svaha.

Which alludes to paying respect to the *Shakti* of desire and nailing it down.

This penetrating and marvelous power is in an arrow whose manifestation is the goddess Rajni.

It is a mantra of the highest degree which can take one to *Shivahood.*

Her *yantra* is a hexagonal form which is produced by juxtaposition of two triangles:

The upward pointing triangle symbolizes the male aspect of the supreme reality

And the downward pointing triangle symbolizes its female aspect, *Shakti.*

Thus the total hexagonal shape symbolizes the eternal unity of *Shiva-Shakti.*

Each arm of the triangles represent her *gunas: Tamasi, Rajasi,* and *Sattvika.*

The hexagonal space formed by the two triangles is the seat of the goddess,

Which is protected by the six Kashmiri deities.

The hexagonal star is enclosed by a circle which represents the cyclical cosmic forces.

The circle blossoms into eight lotus petals, signifying the unfolding of the divine essence.

The *yantra* has further architecture of other geometric shapes,

The journey through which leads the tantric *sadhaka*

To the *bindhu* (center of the *yantra),* where the goddess resides, carrying in her the supreme consciousness.

The whole representational concept of the *yantra* is the integration of a person with cosmos,

Releasing the latent energy in the human system for a cosmic bliss.

She came all the way from Lanka to Kashmir to start a new life:
Ravana, the great demon of Lanka, a great devotee of Shiva and a yogi, but still a *Tamasi*,
Did a dedicated penance for a hundred thousand years but found that he was still not favored by gods.
In distress he prayed to Brahama, who responded to him and told him
To worship *Shakti* from that point on for his good.
Ravana prayed to her for ten thousand years and she finally appeared before him.
Impressed, the goddess *Shyama/ Tripurasundari* bestowed on him the kingdom of Lanka
And assured him that it will last for three eons and gifted him a boon:
Ravana asked for the goddess to live in his house, so that she is always near him.
She accepted his request and stayed in his house for a long time but then got turned off
By the regular demonic rituals of the offerings of buffalos, alcohol, and humans
And furthermore when Ravana threatened to kill Rama to keep Sita with him,
She decided to leave Lanks and move on to *Satidesha* (Kashmir).
Shiva Bhairavi mandated her to take care of Kashmir Valley and
Rama, her devotee, asked Hanuman to take her there, accompanied by countless *nagas.*

Crossing Pir Panjal mountain in Kashmir, she went to Kapalamula, Vishnupada, Madhyagrama,
Khilavar ini, Anantanaga, Lokutpur, Rayasthal, Vadipur, Kotipur, Chandipur,
Tankarpur, and Sharda (Teethwal, now in Pakistan).
Finally, she selected a marshy area, near the confluence of rivers Sindh and Vitasta,
Which was suitable for *nagas* and was studded with trees.
Tulmul became her home and the foremost *mandala.*

The beginnings of the Khir Bhavani temple are shrouded in mystery:
Tulmul residents used to pay homage to a natural spring which was surrounded by marshes.
One day, in the last quarter of the 19th Cent., the village mystic, Pandit Govid Joo Gadru,
Had a vision of a goddess, who manifested herself as a serpent,
Dwelling at a spot at the marshes.
He felt her presence at that spot;
It was confirmed by another village wise man, Krishna Taplu.
Emergence of Maharajni Khir Bhavani at Tulmal soon became history.

She rose from the level of a *Tamasi* goddess at Lanka to *Sattvika* state in Kashmir
Through her yogic power and willfulness.
She showed the people that a person can achieve excellence
With the right spirit and the right guidance.
She also echoed the virtue of mobility when necessary.

Khir Bhavani came to Kashmir when its people were drifting hopelessly,
Having lost their great visions, faith, and discipline.
Kashmiri Pandits are again in confusion and spiritual distress,
They need a leap of mind to reignite their faith and galvanize their practical skills,
And find the path forward.

THE ANGUISH OF KASHMIRI PANDITS

Walking down the fossilized time,
Revisiting high pinnacles and green lakes
Of spirituality and learning,
Today the old native of Kashmir,
Kicked out of his natural habitat,
Wanders the far corners of the world–
To start a new life, a new community;
To heal his wounds, to follow the old light.

Cut off from its spiritual center,
The community wanders in silent grief,
To find a mooring,
To revive the luminosity that once brightened its universe,
To rekindle the fire that bound it together.
But unable to be reborn,
It gradually drifts into the unnamed universal melting pot,
Turning its hallowed past into history,
Its vision into yet unborn hopes.

THE GLORY AND THE EXILE

As far as we can look back in the recorded history of Kashmir,
We see a river of Hindus flowing through thousands of years;
Even beyond the recorded history they are thought to have been
there.
Five-thousand years of time is some weight for claiming their
ancestral
Lineage in their land–a claim that now pierces like a dagger
through their heart.

The name Kashmir is found in unbroken form in ancient Hindu
texts:
Nilmatpurana, Ashtadhyayi, Mahabarta, Puranas, and Braht
Samhitta.
We know of Gonandiya Dynasty's continuous reign over
three-thousand years.
Legend has it that King Gonanda The First and his son Damodra
Lost their lives fighting in Kureva–Pandava war of Mahabarta.

After thousands of years of Hindu civilization,
Under the new Buddhist convert, King Ashoka,
Buddhism took over Kashmir for the next few hundred years.
It was then the city of Srinagri, later moved and renamed Srinagar,
was founded.
Fourth international Buddhist Council was held in Kundalvan
(Harwan),

In which five-hundred scholars from different countries participated.

Mahayana Buddhism was born there.

Kashmir become the preeminent center of Buddhism,

From where it diffused to Central Asia, Tibet, China, Korea, and Japan.

Lord Buddha is himself supposed to have felt that Kashmir was the right place for meditation.

In seventh century the renowned Chinese monk Hiuen Tsiang stayed here for two years.

For two-thousand years Kashmir was an incandescent source of Sanskrit learning and literature.

It had the intellectual culture to dwell on the deepest human connections

To God, immortality, consciousness, human values, and the mode of living.

It produced some of the most fecund and luminous scholars:

Kalhan, Bilhan, Acharya Bhamba, Udbhata, Acharya Kutanka, Mammata,

Anand Vardhana, Vamana, Rudrata, Kshemendra, Rojanak Shitianth.

A star would light in the firmament whenever Abhinav Gupta meditated alone on Kahmir Shaivism.

The most tragic point in Kashmir Pandits' history came in 1339,

When Shah Mir founded the Shamiri dynasty paving the way

For seven-hundred years of Muslim rule in Kashmir.

Their torture and humiliation reached its peak under

The fifth Sultan Sikandar, who imposed a tax, *jiziya,*

On people who happened to be Pandits, and banned their use of *tilak.*

Brutally wounded and hounded, so many Pandits left Kashmir that a legend

That only eleven families were left behind was engendered.

As if they had not borne enough suffering they had to endure another
Cycle of torture and humiliations under Pathans and Sikhs.

With India's independence new hopes rose among the Pandits
That their better days were not far off.
In the beginning *Naya Kashmir* sounded a bugle of fairness and freedom,
Only to be dashed by the new wave of discriminations.
New Delhi heavily invested in keeping the Muslims happy,
At the huge deficit of Pandits' economic security and advancement.

Pakistan hungered for Kashmir from the first moment of its creation.
When the beloved did not return its suitor's attentions enough,
It used the ultimate weapon of religious unity and succeeded somewhat.
An insurgency much planned by Zia of Pakistan materialized in 1989,
Killing one thousand Pandits and leaving them no recourse but to leave Kashmir.
About forty-thousand of them still miserably languish in the refugee camps of Jammu.
But Pandits' plight has still not moved the GOI–
Engendering a new expression: refugees in their own country.

The supreme irony of Kashmiri Pandits is that today they are asked who they are?
Being a minority in the present cycle of history,
Politicians wonder if it is absolutely necessary for them to live in Kashmir.
How would the architect of Taj Mahal have felt
If his name were omitted from the history of the monument?
Today's Kashmiri Pandit is a refugee trying desperately to hold on to his identity;

He is all over the world, trying to continue his ethos.
The community is like scattered leaves in search of the tree they
were shaken off from,
Or the stones of a temple demolished by terrorists
Trying to join with each other to re-form the original shrine.

Pandits are beating their chest on what has happened:
They lived poorly in Kashmir but they were in their home;
They were heavily discriminated against but it did not matter.
But now out of their historical and cultural womb,
Exiled in their and foreign lands,
They feel the earth is shaking under their feet–
They see the signs of their civilization coming to an end.
Many efforts are being made to preserve their ethos
But the forces of diffusion are strong and they are on the wrong
side of history.
It is still difficult to murmur the words that Kashmiri Pandit
community is dead,
But their thoughtful are preparing for that.

When the history of Kashmiri Pandits is written fifty years from
now,
It will be noted with irony and pain
That there was a community in the fabled land of Kashmir who
For five-thousand years there reached high levels of philosophy,
religion, and literature;
Who were peace-loving and deeply immersed in religion;
And who were forced to leave their homeland for political
reasons.
And their subsequent painful diaspora and diffusion all over the
world
Thinned their original personality and culture so much
That their civilization became extinct.
And the history of a thousand-year tormented community came
to a tranquil end,

But their story will inspire many a mind and warm many a heart.

But Pandits know that their end in this world, at this time, is not their end in the universe,
Because the universe has no beginning and no end,
What has been created by God once lives forever,
Their spirit is enshrined in eternity.

They will be reborn when the present cycle of Indian history is over,
They will reclaim their paradise and live there as they have always done.

AGONY OF DAL LAKE

A stunningly beautiful woman,
Robed in ample, majestic mountains,
Crowned with soaring peaks.
A sublime mother, who for eons has nourished her children,
A cosmic *sanyasin,* who has meditated
For a few million years to be in God's feet–
That is Dal Lake.

I am in a *shikara* surfing the soothing waters of Dal Lake.
After twelve years of exile in U.S. I have come to visit her,
To rejuvenate our relationship, to put back my mind on fire.
But at this moment I feel blown off my feet
In the beautiful agony of meeting my beloved,
After an inhuman lapse of time.

I see from my *shikara* a scintillating, pulsating expanse of water,
Touching the faraway sinewy shimmering shores.
The dance of the wavelets produced by the *shikara*
And caressing cool breeze sets an invisible opera.
This is even before I have set my eyes above the water surface.
What did God have in mind when he created Dal Lake?
Did he want to help Kashmiris with an abundant supply of
Water, cool air, flowers, fish, and vegetables?
Or did he want to create a supremely beautiful place
Which would mesmerize people to believe in a higher meaning of life?

We do not know God's thoughts
But we guess he wanted to do both the things:
He wanted to help his creation in both the physical and spiritual spheres.
But still the overall mystery of Dal Lake is inscrutable:
When and how was it created
And how long will it remain here?

The mountains circumferencing the lake are magnificent.
Their light brown color is sensuously stylish.
They seem to be eternally protecting Dal Lake's privacy,
Cradling a spectrum of gardens in their fluid folds,
A semi-circular ring hugs the lake tightly.
The two islands, Sona Lank and Rupa Lank,
Are two more ornaments embellishing the lake.

Like a celestial visitor, Hari Parbat
Stands in a serene majesty and mystery on the west of the lake–
A part of the whole scene, yet apart from it.
On the south-west, like a sentinel, rises
Shankaracharya mountain and the temple.
Very foreign to the lake but yet blending with its ensemble.

In the distant western background lies the Pir Panchal mountain,
Behind the Zabarwan Mountains skirting the lake,
Stands the awesome Himalayan range in distance,
Making the big picture of Dal Lake huge and complex.
Looking atop Shankaracharaya it is a vast canvass
Brushed with haphazard clusters of dwellings,
Water bodies, and mountains.
There is a mystic quality to the scene:
It seems to have been made by design and with a purpose.
It is so close to us but yet so remote from us.

Dal Lake, including all its tributaries, seen from above
Looks like a baby in a fetal position.
Each of its components: Gagribal, Lokut Dal, Bud Dal, and Nagin

Are special entities but it is the whole, the Dal Lake, which has
The spellbinding charisma, the soul, and the magic.

The Moghul Gardens have gained a legend, an aura, and fame
over Dal Lake.
This is an unfortunate and egregious development–
Staining the truth, squelching the facts.
Moghul Gardens are some 300 years old,
Not upgraded for a long time, crassly ignored in maintenance.
They do not stand much against the world-class gardens.
If it were not for the beautiful mountains behind them
And the stunningly magnificent lake in front of them
They would not be worth writing home about.

What is Srinagar without Dal Lake–
A dirty, disheveled medieval town,
Needing much order and repair.
Any discriminating observer when thinking of Srinagar
Would first think of Dal Lake and its environs.

Shikara-riding the lake opens new scenes of beauty in every direction.
From the shimmer of water and melody of oars drumming it
To the dancing breeze that unrehearsedly greets you,
You find yourself in another universe,
Without an agenda and without a care.
You are transformed from a careful, trained observer
To a consciousness in daze, intoxication, and state of freedom,
In increasing gradations.
You are in a state of a dream,
Drifting from scenic discovery to self-discovery,
Drowned in a half-ecstasy created by the sublime ethereality of the lake,
Wanting to die now and here–
Which would be a crowning achievement
For man's heroic struggle to survive in an ugly world.
We do not know if there is a heaven
But we know that Dal is close to it.

Look at the lake at sunrise and at sunset,
In spring and in summer,
In fall and in winter,
In morning and in evening–
In each setting the lake has a special beauty,
A unique mood.
Like a ravishingly beautiful woman,
It is not one beauty that she possesses
But several, depending upon external circumstances.
While her beauty changes she is still the same:
An ever evolving and yet an ever constant maiden.

As if God had not created an amazing enough phenomenon,
He also created the *rads*–the floating lands in the lake.
They move and can be even stolen.
They are home to vegetables, flowers, and fowl,
Creating a human touch in the tapestry of God.

Have you been on the lake on a summer evening,
When the setting sun paints the horizon golden red?
At that time the dividing road between the Bud Dal and Lokut Dal
Gets transformed into scintillating silhouette
And the whole scene gets imbued with some divine meaning.

The memories of the old life in Kashmir
Flash bringing in the family trips on the lake in a *doonga.*
For the poverty-drenched life of those days
Such interludes provided the much needed romance of life.

But our ecstasy turns sour,
As Dal Lake is immensely polluted at this time.
Due to its neglect over long haul of time it has
Sediments, poor water quality, weed growth, encroachments.
It has shrunk from 8.5 sq. mi. to 6.9.
A resplendent lake with pristine waters

Has turned into a polluted body of water
And is in a shocking state of disrepair.
The angelically beautiful woman has been
Beaten, harassed, starved, and compromised.

Today Dal Lake moans in pains unnameable,
Cursing its unworthy sons and daughters,
Who besides neglecting her
Have turned the God's Valley into
A political inferno and ignited a religious war.
They have robbed the smiles from the children's faces
And spun them into decades of trauma.
They have divided the two communities
With such brutality that they will remain apart
For generations to come.
The lake mourns the wasting of God's gift of Kashmir
To its crass inhabitants.
In utter sorrow Dal Lake does not know what to do:
Should it disappear or shrink to an insignificant pond?
Only the invisible arrow of time will tell.

Sanyasin–a religious devotee seeking God
Shikara–a small hand paddled boat
Rad–floating pieces of land

IRREPRESSIBLE YOUTH
The Reminiscences Of Amar Singh College Years

Amar Singh College was a big college lying on the south-west of Srinagar,
It is close to Wazir Bagh and Amira Kadal and on one end and Jehlum river flood canal on the other.
Amir Kadal has been the 5th Ave. of Srinagar for generations and will continue to do so till
Suburban development in Srinagar comes of age.
But the college was considered a few notches lower to S.P. College,
The third college of its day in the city.
Amar Singh College was equipped with sprawling grounds
Wrapped in suburban dignity and tranquility.

In fifties when I was a student there the college atmosphere was highly conservative:
Students were keenly deferential to professors and subservient to management.
Only in the college tuck-shop and the playgrounds their inhibitions melted.
Education was nothing but passing of the exams,
Sports were not a hot attraction then
And girls were more an idea than reality.
But with all its unsophistication it was still fun to be there.

Prof. J,N. Dhar taught physics with a tyrannical control of the classroom.

He threw temper tantrums at will.

He could throw a student out of the classroom for the slippage from the expected competence or etiquette.

One day he doused a student's head with cold water to make him behave better;

Another day when a student tried to defend himself against the professor's accusations in studied English,

He retorted back, "I need an explanation and not literature."

But he knew what he was teaching.

Prof. Nand Lal Darbari was a senior professor of chemistry

But a popular butt of jokes due to his comic appearance and handling of things.

Once when Principal Mahmood Ahmed had to go on a vacation,

Due to his seniority, Prof. Durbari had to fill in, something he did not like to do.

Among the very first tasks he had to perform as an Acting Principal

Was to approve a long absence from college application from a student.

The student arrived with the application in his office and explained

The reason for his request, which was his sister's marriage.

Prof. Durbari was annoyed that he was the one who had to handle such a request

And told the student, "Did your sister have to get married when I am an Acting Principle?"

Another time Prof. Durbari arrived in the class after an absence of a week,

Due to his son's marriage. He sat on the table, with legs dangling, in his customary manner.

A student shouted at him, asking what was the menu at his son's marriage reception.

Prof. Darbari went through the list of the items on the menu
And when he finished reading the item *gulabjamun,*
The student slammed back, "Professor, you look like a *gulabjamun.*"
Ever since the nickname *gulabjamun* stuck.

Prof. Yusuf Jandugar taught physics,
He was flamboyant, unsophisticatedly straight, and authoritarian.
He was thin like a reed, tall, and wore a *pagadi.*
Explaining make and break positions of an electrical device
He would elaborate on the make position of the device at one wall of the classroom
And then walk to the opposite wall to explain its changing to the break position.
When he spoke, students listened with complete attention,
Because of the absolute fear they had of him.
He told the class one day that it was alright to swindle, as long as it was for a large sum of money.
To escape the handcuffs all one had to do is hire an expensive lawyer from England.

Prof. J.N. Kaul taught English.
Though he was of small-build he was feared.
He used to wear a *Gandhi* cap and limped in one leg.
He gave us a class, on a certain day of the week, at 9:00 A.M.–
It was the first class of the day.
On this particular day he was running late.
All the students were waiting for him on the second floor verandah,
From where there was a clear view of the college bicycle shed,
Where he was going to park his bicycle.
Lo and behold he could be sighted,
Pumping his bicycle pedals furiously.
As he reached the bicycle shed, he quickly alighted from the bicycle,
Swiftly giving it to the shed attendant.

247

Then he strode, like a tiger, toward the college building.

As the momentum of his stride increased, his sight became very compelling.

Suddenly, I heard some students singing, *badta chal, badta chal, taroon ke hath pakdta chal . . .*

This was a refrain from a song of a popular movie, Boot Polish (?),

But as soon as he reached close to the building, the students suddenly stopped singing.

I have another memory of Prof. J.N.Kaul:

Just before his class it was announced that *Sadarariyast* Karan Singh was in the process

Of making a surprise visit to the college.

Prof. warned us to be ready for it.

Lo and behold Karan Singh with his entourage entered our class.

He had a big smile on his face and asked the professor about what we were studying.

Then he asked him who was the shining star of his class.

I felt nervous as I thought I was that person.

To my utter shock the professor just beat about the bush for a few moments

And then announced that there was no shining star in his class.

I could not forgive him for that.

Later, I realized why he did not indicate who the best student was:

It was because of the fear that the best student might have tripped Karan Singh's questions,

Thereby, blemishing professor's image.

Prof. S.P. Bakhshi would dress immaculately, was well mannered, and a bachelor.

He taught us chemistry.

He was famous for his statement on why he remained a bachelor:

Jab dood milta hai, gai lane ki kya zaroorat hai.

In English it means: when you are assured of a supply of milk, why buy a cow.

Prof. Yousuf taught us Charles Dickens' A Tale Of Two Cities.
He would read the text verbatim in his terrible pronunciation:
He pronounced the character Larry as Lorry, the Kashmiri word
for a bus.
After reading every few lines he would warn us: mark humor,
mark drama, mark action, . . .

Because of the shortage of the girls each girl was special.
God has bestowed on us three at one time.
Indu Raina and Sheela Thussu, Roll Numbers 8 and 303, were
my classmates.
Indu was tall and well-built, while Sheela was slender and of
common proportions.
The former was moderately sociable, while the latter was properly so,
Within the social taboos of the age.
Each day boys would keenly wait for them to arrive in the class
And examine them top to bottom for their attires and moods.
Their smiles were our happinesses; their grey moods were our
sorrows.
I nicknamed Sheela, three-not-three, based on her roll number,
Which stuck somewhat.

One day Abdul Ahad, physics demonstrator, called me to his desk,
Just at the beginning of our physics lab.
I was smitten with fear for it was unusual to be called like that.
Abdul Ahad told me that since Sheela Thussu had called sick
I would have to partner with Indu Raina in the experiment as
apparatuses were limited.
I became very nervous with the thought of spending eight hours
with a girl
In front of the whole class and the demonstrator.

Within seconds the entire class came to know of my situation;
Boys threw mischievous smiles on me,
For they thought I was in for a great time for the rest of the day.
I was unable to tell them that I was feeling miserable.

Within minutes Indu and I had to stand in front of
The sound velocity measurement by the tuning fork method
apparatus.
Indu was taking the lead and I was coyly following her.
Hours passed and we were not getting any results.
It was clear to me, and I guess to her, that our nervousnesses were
the culprits.

Boys inundated me with comments suggesting what a lucky bum
I was.
They would not take my assertions of the horrible time I was
having.
After the break we resumed our work with lesser nervousness
and obtained some good results.
At the end of the day we were relieved that the torture was
over–
The quality of our work was inconsequential.
After some days I felt that in spite of the torture I had
experienced
The experience had some sublimity to it–
A romantic languor hung over me for months.
One day the news came that Sheela was ill and would be away
from college for a long time:
She never returned.

The teaching and the whole architecture of preparing students for
higher studies was preposterous.
Classroom lectures were mostly professorial monologues,
Mechanically listened to by the students,
While their hearts and minds were focused on something else.
They knew that all they had to do to pass the exam was
To start opening the books just three months before the exams.
So, why should they put effort to understand and retain what was
being taught now.
Going to college to learn was a big sham: one could have easily
stayed home and learnt more.

The education system was a grand cultural fraud, perpetuated from generation to generation.
Students just crammed the likely materials questioned in the exams,
To just pass the exams, which was done to get the jobs.
There was no learning and no character building.

Preparing for exams, which would fall during the two month winter vacation,
Was the highest ordeal of studying.
Students would mug and mug during days and parts of the nights.
Some would get up at 4:00 AM to study.
If overpowered by sleep they would douse their heads under a cold tap.
Understanding the subject material was less important than its memorizing.
Students would turn into memory machines.
Families would get fully involved with the enterprise.
They would see to it that teas, meals, *kangaris*, etc. were provided.
To get a relief from stress students would refresh themselves by taking walks.
By the examination time the stress level would have risen very high.
In my neighborhood a boy from a milk-seller family almost suffered a breakdown:
His appearance and talk changed as the exams approached.

Fridays were half-days due to Muslims' need to go to a mosque.
A few willful students would make rounds of their friend circle
And ask for two *paisas*, which was all they said they needed to complete the
Seven-and-half *annas* they needed to buy a third-class movie ticket.

Many friends would spare two *paisas,* as this meager amount would let
Their friend see a movie, which was the highest level entertainment available those days.
Later we would find that the boys did not have any money at all to begin with–
By collecting fifteen two *paisas* they would realize their dream, using mendacious means.

There used to be four girls studying in our rival college, S.P. College.
Boys had nicknamed them: *Badal, Garja, Bijli,*and *Chamki,* keyed to their personalities.
Which in English mean: Cloud, Thunder, Lightning, and Flash.
When I was in the third year *Chamki* moved to our college,
To the great excitement of the boys.
There were two other girls who also moved to our college from somewhere.
They came with their nicknames, Chunnu and Munnu.
I ran for some election in the third-year student body,
For which I had to canvass, including flesh-pressing.
But my acute shyness prevented me from approaching Chunnu and Munnu.
The loss of two votes in this close election was crucial but my hands were tied.

But toward the end of the canvassing period I was surprised to see the two girls
Approach me, while I was standing in a verandah.
I became nervous, not knowing how to handle myself,
But there was no way I could run away from the impending encounter.
Confrontation finally happened. Chunnu, the petite, slightly chubby girl, my favorite out of the two,
After looking around to make sure no one was watching us, told me that they were going to vote for me.

My excitement at this, mixed with my agitated nervousness, made me just blabber a thank you.

Chunnu emboldened by delivering her message and seeing my nervousness, next asked me
If I needed anything else from her?
Hearing this from her my eyes almost popped out.
I tried to tell Chunnu what I wanted from her but my voice choked and my hands started to tremble.
Looking at my utter misery the girls gave me a tantalizingly mischievous smile and walked away from me.
I vowed to myself right then that I would never again run for an election which would have a women electorate;
And I have kept that promise.

F.Sc. practical exam in chemistry was under way:
There was a lot of tension because here was a test
Where mugging could do only so much.
Results had to be produced under the eyes of the examiner
And then one had to go through viva voce with him.
My examiner was Prof. Nasserullah, a very handsome, well-dressed, and friendly guy.
I did not do badly in the experiment but my shyness was a block
I had to negotiate in the viva.
To my utter shock Prof. Nasserullah's first question to me was: which was my latest movie?
After easily answering that question, his next question was: who was my favorite actress?
Emboldened by the answer to the first question I did not mind saying that it was Madhubala–
An answer I would not have normally given because of my shyness and inhibitions of the times,
As Madhubhala was a sexy woman.
That was the end of the viva, there were no technical questions.
I was relieved beyond my imagination.
In the evening my uncle by chance met the professor during the after-office stroll in Amira Kadal,

And asked him how I fared in the exam;
The professor replied that I was very nervous but there was
nothing to be worried about.

Physics practical exam was easier;
Someone in my family, without informing me,
Informed Prof. Triloki Nath Kilam, the examiner,
That I would be taking an exam under him.
Prof. Kilam and we were relatives.
Following day in the lab the tensions were expectedly high.
We waited anxiously as Prof. Kilam walked into the lab:
He was good looking, properly-dressed, and under pressure.
After a few moments he walked across the lab and in his famous
Way of peering over his glasses, whispered in my ears: are you
Zind Lal Kaul's son?
After I nodded he abruptly broke away from me.
Rest of the time in lab was just going though the exam.
But when the results came, I was just awarded about twenty-some
marks out of the forty–
A very mediocre rating; it was clear to me that my relative had
not given me any bonus
Because of our relationship.

The college tuck shop was a buzz of excitement:
Students smoking, drinking tea, talking uninhibitedly about girls
and professors.
There was also talk about movies and politics.
Overcome by the good time they were having,
Many times students would cut their classes.
But the image of the tuck shoppers was bad;
They were considered poor students, drop-outs, irresponsible,
and low-level.
And, of course, it was off-limits to girls.

The grounds at the college were open, smooth, serene, and
semi-secluded.

Many an hour have I spent looking at them and the associated horizon,
To escape the humbug and the clamor of the world;
They gave me much needed enchanted loneliness.
Friends would sit down under a *chinar* and survey the universe;
We savored moments of delicious gossip and searing conversation.
I spent innumerable hours playing cricket here.
Many classes in summer and early fall would be outdoors, on the grounds.
If there was only one thing I was allowed to remember about the college,
It would be the life on its grounds.

With all the mediocrity of the education provided at the college,
There was still a music ringing in one's soul:
Of the majesty of life, the wonder of nature, the beckoning of the unknown.
Life appeared infinitely rich—an enterprise conceived by the gods;
It seemed to be a calling of very high magnitude,
Everything was touched by grandeur,
Everything was eternal.
With all the life that has flown down since
Nothing has matched the magic of those years.

Nadir Monjays At Tarakh Halwoy's Shop

Evening has assumed a serene yet exciting mood,
Everything is pregnant with tranquil hopefulness
After day's shattering struggle with survival;
To make money men would stress themselves to death.

I have worn the best night suit I have
And carefully disheveled my hair in a Dilip Kumar coiffure
And slipped the best *khaddaoon* we had in the house.
Off I go to Tarak Halwoy's sweet shop
To have a good time.

Tarakh Halwoy's sweet shop is near Habba Kadal,
An elite shopping center of Srinagar.
It is a small, dark and dingy place.
Full of cooking utensils,
With little room for the customers to sit and eat.
Tarakh Halwoy himself is rotund and mouth-shut,
Continuously busy cooking sweets in a big kadai,
Never bantering with his customers.

Maybe, it was the first take-out in Kashmir.
The shop serves *nadir munjays, dodhu alavs, pakoras, samosas,*
Puris, seemniy, burfi, ladoos, pedas, and other things–
All high delicacy Kashmiri snacks.
Although the place is renowned for its *dodhu alavs*

But *nadir munjays* give me a gastro-delight high.

The scene outside the shop is that of crushing high traffic,
With *tangawallahas* exhorting their emaciated horses with voice
and whip,
In the nightmarishly narrow lanes panicky pedestrians scrambling
for their safety
And sometimes colliding with the shop walls.
The scene is soaked with chaos, fear, noise, and excitement.
But those were the sounds and the sights we would want to
experience
When visiting Tarakh Halwoy.
In those days of youth, primitiveness, and poverty,
Habba Kadal was our Times Square and Tarakh Halwoy was our
Macdonald's.

Besides the delectations at Tarakh Halwoy's sweet shop
There were delectations at the street in front of it to be had:
Sweet, nimble, love-filled girls walking toward Habba Kadal,
Pretending not to look at Dilip Kumars in the sweat shop
But yet stealing full amorous glances at them,
Contoured with caressing sexy half-smiles.

My visit to Tarakh Halwoy's sweet shop was just an excuse
To have a chance to see Bimla, my dancing heart-throb,
With whom my eyes-only romance
Had been born on the neighboring Habba Kadal bridge,
On which we would walk round and round,
Though in opposite directions of traffic,
With our gazes inter-locked,
Till the street cops and the stray animals
Would look at us with angry suspicion.
Much have I fantasized to share Nadir Munjays
One day with Bimla at the sweet ship.

1. *khadaoon*: wooden casual footwear

2. *nadir monjayas, dodhu alavs, pakoras, samosas, puris, seemniy, burfi, ladoos, pedas, dodhu alavs* all are popular Kashmiri snacks

3. *tangawallahas:* operators of horse-driven carriages

A RENDEZVOUS AT HABBA KADAL

Today, I have laid out my new night suit on the bed,
After carefully ironing it with rice starch.
Also, I have spit-polished my leather shoe to its best wet shine.
Both to be worn late in the afternoon to visit Habba Kadal.
Habba Kadal is the Third Bridge on River Jehlum, in Srinagar.
It is a hub of commercial and social activity.
Filled with grocery vendors, bookshops, and general merchandise shops.
Dr. Chagtoo, a prominent physician, has an office there.

During the day Habba Kadal is a busy town square,
In the early evenings it takes more of a social stage.
Men and women, boys and girls come out here to
Buy things, to converse, and often just to see and be seen.
Young people come to meet their gender opposites for a whiff of a romance,
Superficial in happenings yet real in desire, longing, and hope.

I donned my new night suit with elegant ease
And combed my hair with thick linseed cooking oil,
Creating a lustrous curl-flip rising from the forehead
And dancing down to the mid-ridge.
I marched with controlled excitement for a chance rendezvous with Bimla,
Who schools at the neighboring Vasanta Girls High School,
Where my aunt is the Headmistress.

We met once fleetingly at the school picnic.
She is coy and serene, self-conscious and lovelorn.
She took considerable pains to avoid meeting my continuous
gaze on her.
We have never talked and never written to each other
But yet it seems to me an invisible candle has been lit between us.

Today, at four-thirty in the afternoon, I joined a throng of boys
Lined up on one side of the bridge, waiting for the bevy of girls to
Walk on the other side.
Here were two groups, separated by gender,
Who had come to see each other
But pretended to be out on some errand.

The corresponding gazes of each couple locked in
While their legs just carried them on.
Occasionally, the couples looked ahead of themselves
To give a semblance of a regular bridge crossing.
Not surprisingly the people bumped into each other
When losing track of what was ahead of them.

The bridge romance was as real as a romance could be
Those days in Kashmir.
Love surge of youth had to find an outlet,
Circumventing the terrible taboos of the day.
God created love but man created morality.
Like a summer brook love found grooves and byways
To flow and flood the virgin ground before it.

I searched for Bimla in the crushing stream of girls.
After an infinite waiting I finally found her pair of eyes
And held them into an eternal lock with mine after her response.
Mesmerized thus the two of us walked the entire bridge
Like two zombies lost to this world.

The time thus passed seemed unbounded
And the place we were at did not exist.

The end of the bridge ended our trance
As the paths following it were divergent,
Breaking our gazes, ending the romantic rendezvous.
Afterward, I folded my night suit with diligent dexterousness
For the next gaze-crossing
And wondered how would my unbearable romantic tension end.

Years rolled by and I never met Bimla's eyes again.
I heard she was married and lived happily not far from the bridge.
I also now wonder if she knew my name.
Much as I muse about my run with the flame,
I realize that all I am left with now is a pair of eyes.

Upon Waking Up On My Birthday

I woke up on my birthday to find out when the *guruji* will arrive,
To perform the *pooja* invoking the gods for my well being.
I waited for the refreshing rub of a new shirt
And the gastronomical seduction of *tahar and charvan*.
The dignifying touch of a *tilak* was missing,
So was the mysterious bond of a *narivan*.
All of these are now interesting relics in the museum of time.
Most of us did not understand then,
And even now, what these sanctified trappings were for.
But we felt we were being connected to something larger than us,
Something within us but beyond the ordinary reach.
Every age has its rituals but birthdays will always have the same message:
To celebrate life and to feel its miracle.

guruji	priest
pooja	religious ceremony
tahar	salted yellow rice, which must be served with yogurt after the ceremony
charvan	goat or lamb liver cooked as a hot, spicy curry
tilak	a vermilion paste mark on the forehead, between the eyes. Bears high religious connection
Narivan	a red and white twisted cotton thread tied on the wrist by the priest after the ceremony. Religious connection

ROOTS

Touching the ground on which I put the first shaky footsteps,
Seeing the majestic contours of the undulating skyline,
Which my eyes had never tired to range,
Back in Kashmir, I feel the echo of my genesis–
An expatriate's answered prayers.

Buried here lie the pristine years of my childhood,
When wonder turned into thought,
Desires into dreams,
The visions was uncluttered,
And conflict took root.

Does a man owe something to the land of his birth,
Or is it his insecurity that binds him to his roots?
Or is it all an alluring angle of the architecture of emotion,
Or simply an elemental pull to gravitate to one's origin?
If child is the father of man, then what is growing up all about?

Unblemished by the coarseness of life,
Unmarred by the waywardness of the world,
Reposed in the frozen perspective of time,
Still gleaming lie the first experiences of life:

The integrity of self,
The uniqueness of the individual and the brotherhood of mankind,
The uncomplicatedness in human relationships,

Maharaj Kaul

The simplicity of understanding,
The unquestioned joy of living,
The clarity of the way ahead,
Just being, not becoming.

We go back to the roots,
To replenish the vision and the spirit we have lost,
To regain our identity and reclaim our history,
To reset the balance between nature and mind,
To feel an element of the universal spacetime.

But the chilling vision shattered the trip down the childhood:
Kashmiris living the fossilized glory of their past,
Apathy their unshakable creed,
Cynicism the only energetic hope,
Living between tyranny and anarchy of political pendulum.

Walking down the desolate ruins of Srinagar's streets,
Shapeless stretches of thoughtless construction,
Chaotic services and nightmarish traffic,
Where time has frozen in the inner city,
And darkness envelopes the winter months.

Plundered, ravaged, and defiled through ages,
By its soulless bandit rulers,
Neglected eternally by its crass inhabitants,
To wither slowly in the irreversible arrow of time,
This bounteous gift of nature, Kashmir,
Moans in pains unnameable,
Its soul heaving with curse eternal
For its unworthy sons.

The clandestine evil schemes of 80's
Hatched in some hostile country
Coalesced into one infernal insane fire in '89,

Destroying the finely woven culture of a millennia in the valley,
Disturbing the tranquility of a million years among the mountains.

A friend turned into a murderer,
A neighbor into an arsonist;
A community acquiesced to become an army.
An angelic valley became a death valley—
All in the name of God and religion.

We do not know where to begin anew—
Even, if we should begin at all,
To resume God's work,
To revive the spontaneous sparkling smile
On the faces of a thousand gloomy children,
To let the lotuses grow unperturbed.

We do not know what to do—
Our enemy's brutality has choked our spirit,
Their hatred has tormented our soul.
In one cataclysmic insanity
They have destroyed the Kashmir built by Gods.

But Kashmir always beckons me to homecoming,
A quivering echo of a distant thunder,
A withered glow on the horizon,
Remnant of a fire kindled a long time ago,
It will remain my tombstone.